The Wind in the Willows

A musical

Book and lyrics by
Willis Hall

Music by
Denis King

Based on the story by
Kenneth Grahame

Samuel French — London
New York - Toronto - Hollywood

ISBN 0 573 08070 4

THE WIND IN THE WILLOWS

First presented at the Theatre Royal, Plymouth, and subsequently on a national tour by Duncan C. Weldon and Paul Gregg and Lionel Beeker for Triumph Apollo Productions Ltd, with the following cast of characters:

Water-Rat	Patrick Cargill
Mole	Melvyn Hayes
Badger	Donald Hewlett
Toad	Terry Scott
Alfred the Pantomime Horse	Peter Wiggins and Malcolm Wood
1st Fieldmouse	Paul Ryan
Impish Fieldmouse	Richard Tolan
2nd Fieldmouse	Dee Robillard
Toad's Butler	Allan Stirland
The Constable	Michael Boothe
Judge R. De Veering	Anthony Collin
The Clerk-of-Court	David Dandridge
Enid, the Constable's daughter	Deborah Goodman
A Bargewoman	Judith Street
The Chief Weasel	Robert Aldous
Country-Folk, Wild-Wooders, Ducks, Fieldmice, Rabbits and other various animals	Robert Aldous, Fiona Alexanda, Michael Boothe, Anthony Collin, David Dandridge, Deborah Goodman, Wenda Holland, Christopher Hood, Claudia Lyster, Dee Robillard, Paul Ryan, Allan Stirland, Judith Street, Richard Tolan, Peter Wiggins, Malcolm Wood

Directed by Roger Redfarn
Designed by Finlay James
Musical Director Barry Westcott

SYNOPSIS OF SCENES

ACT I

Scene 1	The River Bank
Scene 2	Toad's Estate
Scene 3	The Open Road
Scene 4	The Wild Wood
Scene 5	Outside Toad Hall
Scene 6	Toad's Bedroom
Scene 7	The Same—some days later
Scene 8	The Village

ACT II

Scene 1	The Courtroom
Scene 2	A Dungeon Cell
Scene 3	The Edge of the Wild Wood
Scene 4	The Canal Bank
Scene 5	Rat's Home
Scene 6	The Secret Passage
Scene 7	Toad Hall

CHARACTERS

Water-Rat
Mole
Badger
Toad
Alfred the Pantomime Horse
1st Fieldmouse
2nd Fieldmouse
3rd Fieldmouse
Hawkins, the butler
Enid, the housemaid
The Constable
Judge R. De Veering
The Clerk-of-Court
A Bargewoman
The Chief Weasel

Villagers, **Wild-Wooders**, **Policemen**, **Ducks**, **Rabbits**, and various other animals

MUSICAL NUMBERS

ACT I

1	**Wind in the Willows**	Enid
2.	**Messing About in Boats**	Rat and Mole
3.	**Travelling Man**	Toad, Rat and Mole
4.	**Poop-Poop!**	Toad, Rat and Mole
5.	**Beware!**	Wild-Wooders
6.	**Taken in Hand**	Badger, Rat and Mole
7.	**Rejoice, Rejoice!**	The Fieldmice
8.	**Talking to Toad**	Rat and Mole
9.	**What's a Friend For?**	Rat
10.	**Poop-Poop! (Reprise)**	Company

ACT II

11.	**Send Him Down**	Toad, Badger, Rat, Mole, Company
12.	**Home**	Enid, Toad
13.	**Hello World**	Toad and Company
14.	**Peep-Peep! (Reprise)**	Constables and Bargewoman
15.	**Taken in Hand (Reprise)**	Badger, Mole, Rat and Toad
16.	**Home (Reprise)**	Company
17.	**Hello World (Reprise)**	Company

The Piano/Vocal Score is available from Samuel French Ltd.

ACT I

Scene 1

The River Bank

A full moon hangs low over a stretch of river which meanders through wooded, grassy banks. An owl hoots nearby. There is a mist hanging over the water while, overhead, the night-sky is clear, star-bright, and welcoming

The Water-Rat enters in a rowing-boat

Rat Ah, this is the life—just me, my boat, and the river… (*He pulls into the bank, ships his oars and savours his surroundings*) Nothing much nicer under the moon—except sleeping, perhaps…

The music steals in behind

…and dreaming dreams… (*He snuggles down in the bottom of the boat and falls instantly asleep*)

A girl, Enid, aged about 18, enters. She is wearing a "summery" 1930s' dress, which not only hints at the warmth of the evening, but also sets the period of our story. She does not notice either the rowing-boat or its occupant

Song 1: Wind In The Willows

Enid

Wind in the willows,
The days of our childhood,
Summertime, wintertime, autumn and spring,
Meadow and thicket and spinney and wildwood,
Thrush in the hedgerow and lark on the wing,
And lark on the wing…

Summon the past and the age we spent dreaming,
Where is the singer and what was his song?
Cool was the stream where the fish lay a-gleaming,
Where now the stream our hearts drifted along?

Wind in the willows,
The days we spent dancing,
Golden is childhood and golden is youth,
Wild was the wildwood and wilder romancing,
Can we look back and tell dreaming from truth,
Tell dreaming from truth…?

Gone are the years when the future was ever,
Gone are the times when we ran hand in hand,
Where is the love we thought nothing would sever?
Life is the hour glass, fast ran the sand.

Wind in the willows,
The days of our childhood,
Summertime, wintertime, autumn and spring,
Meadow and thicket and spinney and wildwood,
Thrush in the hedgerow and lark on the wing,
And lark on the wing…

Enid wanders off

The moon is gone and the sun is up

The Mole emerges from a hole close by the river bank. He is wearing a white apron over a black velvet jacket and he holds a whitewash brush. He doesn't notice the rowing-boat as he looks up at the sky and takes in the summer scene. His forepaws quiver with delight

Mole I say! Oh my! This *is* fine! This is one up on spring-cleaning! This is two up on being down there, underground, scraping and scratching and scrabbling and scrooging! (*He tosses away his brush and apron and does a little leap for joy*) Oh my! Oh my, oh my, oh my!

His final cry has woken the Water-Rat who sits bolt upright in his boat. The two animals regard each other cautiously for a moment

Rat Mole, is it?
Mole Yes—you're Rat?
Rat Yes, that's right.
Mole And would you mind telling me where I am?
Rat Where you are? Why—the river, of course. (*With an inviting sweep of his arm*) Would you care to step in?
Mole (*overwhelmed*) May I?

Rat (*extending a hand*) Lean on that—step lively.

The Mole steps into the boat and takes in his surroundings

Mole Do you know—I've never been in a boat before in all my life.
Rat You've never... well, I...! What *have* you been doing then, all this time?
Mole Is it as nice as all that?
Rat It's the *only* thing. I say! If you've nothing else on hand this morning, why don't we drop down the river together? We could make a day of it?
Mole Oh, *yes*! Can we? (*He rocks the boat in his excitement*) Let's start at once!
Rat Take care! (*He steadies Mole*) Pass me that picnic hamper.
Mole (*doing so*) What's inside it?
Rat Cold chicken. Coldchickencoldtonguecoldhamcoldbeefpickledgherkins-greensaladfrenchrollcresssandsandwichespottedmeatgingerbeer-lemonadestickybuns——
Mole Oh, stop! Stop! This is too much!
Rat Do you think so? I was wondering whether I'd packed enough. Off we go!

The Water-Rat takes up the oars and sculls out into the mainstream

Mole So this is a river?
Rat *The* river.
Mole It must be a bit dull at times—just you and the river?
Rat Never. Otters, kingfishers, dabchicks, moorhens——

The Mole points across at a thickly-wooded area on the river bank

Mole Who lives over there?

The Water-Rat ships his oars again and gazes soberly across at the trees

Rat That's the Wild Wood. We don't go there much, we river-bankers.
Mole Aren't they very nice, the animals that live there?
Rat The squirrels aren't bad. Neither are the rabbits—some of 'em. And then there's Badger, bless him. He lives right in the heart of it, wouldn't live anywhere else. Dear old Badger. Nobody interferes with *him*. They'd better not!
Mole Who *should* interfere with him?

A cloud passes over the sun, casting the river bank into shadow. The Mole follows the Water-Rat's glance and, with them, we are aware of quick, darting movements in the Wild Wood and, as the music steals in behind, we hear a sinister, whispered chorus

Voices (*off*) Weasels and foxes and stoats,
Weasels and foxes and stoats…

But the murmur fades as quickly as it came; the cloud has passed on and the sun is shining again

Rat And that's why we never go into the Wild Wood alone. Be warned.

Mole What lies beyond the Wild Wood?

Rat Down the river, just around the next bend, there's Toad Hall. That's *very* grand.

Mole Who lives there?

Rat Why, Toad himself, of course. Who else! He's even grander—well, thinks he is.

Mole And shall we see him?

Rat If he's got time to see us, we might. That'll be if he isn't into his latest craze. Toad's always mad about something—and if it isn't one thing, it's another. It used to be sailing. Next it was punting. He gave that up when he took up horse-riding—and he gave *that* up when he kept falling off. The last I heard, he'd bought himself a bicycle, and he rides round and round his drive on it, ringing his bell. But it won't last—nothing lasts with Toad——

Badger appears, peering across at them over the river bank

There's Badger now. (*He waves*) Come on, old Badger!

Badger No, thank you. I shan't trouble you now—not if you've got company.

Rat It's only my friend, Mole. Come with us. We're off to pay Toad a visit.

Badger I've more to say to Toad than can be expressed in one short excursion. Mr Toad needs to be taken well in hand—and I haven't the time today to perform *that* task. Some other time, perhaps. Good-day!

Badger slips back out of sight

The Water-Rat and Mole wave to him as he goes

Mole Why doesn't he like Mr Toad?

Rat Toad is inclined to boast. And he can be a bit conceited. And he won't ever listen to reason—all that apart, he's all right, is Toady. You'll soon see for yourself.

The Water-Rat applies himself to the oars again. Mole leans back, blissfully

Mole What a day I'm having!

Rat Of course you are, Moley. Believe me, there is nothing—absolutely nothing—half so much worth doing as simply messing about in boats...

Song 2: Messing About in Boats

(*Singing*) Messing about in boats,
On rivers or streams or moats,
There's nothing quite like it,
Don't hike it, or bike it,
Go messing about in boats.

Rat / **Mole** Messing around in craft,
A rowboat or merely a raft,
There's nothing that's neater,
In-fine-itely sweeter,
Than messing around in craft.
Take a trip,
Choose a cruise,
You've got nothing to lose.

Mole Beg a skiff,
Hail a sail,
Of a time have a wonderful glorious whale.

Rat / **Mole** And go
Messing about in boats.
On rivers or streams or moats,
So give it a go and a yo-ho-ho-ho,
And go messing about in boats,
Messing about in boats.

Rat Here's a tip—talk to me,
You can go out to sea.

Mole Seek a ship—hip-hoo-ray,
When the wind fills the sail,
Climb aboard and away,

Rat / **Mole** And go
Messing about in boats,
Or anything else that floats,
There's no grander pastime,
We'll sing it one last time,
Go messing about in boats,
Go messing about in boats.

And, as they continue smoothly down the river, the Lights fade

Scene 2

Toad's Estate

The Lights come up on a lawn which overlooks the river

Toad, his back to the audience, is deep in a wicker chair. There are two more chairs and a matching table. In the background stands a brand new gypsy caravan, painted canary-yellow picked out with green, and with red wheels

Toad is attended by his butler, Albert Hawkins, who is watching critically as Enid, now wearing housemaid's costume, nervously unloads a jug of lemonade and a glass on to the table. Having done so, she bobs Hawkins a curtsy

Enid The master's elevenses, Mr Hawkins.
Hawkins Elevenses, girl? H'it's two minutes past! New girl, Mr Toad—h'answers to the name of h'Enid. She bites 'er nails, she sniffles—she can't carry a tea-tray 'arf-a-yard without it rattling somethink chronic—she can't *lift* the coal-scuttle—she can't iron, she can't 'ang washing, not for love nor money, not h'according to Cook, *and* she's clumsy——

As Hawkins lists Enid's failings, her shoulders droop and her head sinks lower and lower

But this much I will say, sir: she's a trier, bless 'er—h'and we'll make a 'ousemaid of 'er yet—or my name h'ain't h'Albert 'awkins. Off you go, girl.

Enid, now flushed with pride, her spirits lifted, bobs both of them an energetic curtsy and skips away across the lawn

H'Enid!

Enid freezes

Walk, girl—walk! You don't skip when you're in service!

Enid makes a more decorous exit

Toad's attention is elsewhere: we see him fully for the first time as he leaps to his feet when the Water-Rat and Mole arrive, carrying the picnic hamper

Toad Hooray! I jolly well say! This *is* splendid! Who told you? How did you *know*?

Rat Know what?

Toad Why—that I was just about to send a boat down the river for you, Ratty. With strict instructions that, no matter what, you were to drop everything, no matter where, and come here at once, no matter how. Wasn't I, Hawkins?

Hawkins nods in agreement, then shaking his head in bewilderment, he exits, as Toad continues

You're just the two fellows I wanted.

Rat You haven't even met Mole yet.

Toad Who's Mole?

Mole tugs shyly at Toad's jacket and points at himself

How d'yer do. 'Course you're Mole. Grand little chap. 'Course I've met him.

Rat When?

Toad Just then—when we introduced ourselves. Look here, Ratty, there isn't *time* for all these introductions. You don't know how lucky it is, you turning up like this. Come up to the house and have something. (*To Mole*) Finest house on the entire river—who did you say you were again?

Rat Mole! Mole! The name's Mole!

Toad Don't confuse things. You're Ratty. He's Mole. As I was saying, Mole, before Ratty so rudely interrupted: Toad Hall's the grandest residence there is on the river.

Mole I'm sure that's so.

Toad I'll be delighted to show you over it—after we've had a bite of lunch.

Rat (*throwing himself into a garden chair*) Let's sit quiet a bit, Toady. Besides, there's no need to go up to the house. We've brought a picnic hamper. There's cold chicken——

Rat
Mole (*together*) —coldtonguecoldhamcoldbeefpickledgherkinssaladfrenchrollscresssandwichespottedmeatgingerbeerlemonadesodawater——

Toad Stop! Stop! There isn't time for food either. I need your help—it's most important.

Rat If it's to do with bicycling, Toady, and you want us to watch you riding round and round the drive——

Toad Bicycling? *Bicycling*! Going round and round in circles. Ting-a-ling, ting-a-ling! Bicycling's boring, Ratty. Boring, boring, boring! No—I've discovered the real thing at last. The *only* thing that's really worth doing. The only thing in life, Ratty.

Rat Go on—I'm listening. What is it this time?
Toad What is it? Are you blind? It's staring you in the face.

Rat and Mole follow Toad's glance and take in the caravan. Mole is impressed, Rat is not

Mole It's a caravan!
Toad It's not just *a* caravan, Moley—it's *the* caravan.
Rat I think I'd have rather had the bicycle…

Song 3: Travelling Man

Toad
I have recently discovered,
I'm a travelling man,
There's a world out there,
For a gypsy caravan.
There's the highway,
There's the heath,
There's the open road,
There's the low path,
There's the tow-path,
I'm a nomad toad.

I'm a travelling man,
And the world is mine.
Here today,
Gone tomorrow and the future's fine.
There's the blue sky up above,
There's the earth below,
And a sun to shine upon me,
Wherever I go.

All
La-la-la-la-la-la
La-la-la-la-la
La-la-la
La-la-la-la-la-la-la-la-la.
There's the blue sky up above,
There are fields below,
And the sun to shine down on me,
Wherever I go.

Mole It sounds wonderful.
Toad Come inside. It's got everything that we could possibly need—I planned it all myself.

The excited Mole follows Toad into the caravan. The Rat, unimpressed, digs his hands in his pockets and waits outside, feigning disinterest. Mole's face appears at the caravan window

Mole It's true, Ratty—it *has* got everything. Sleeping bunks, a table that folds up, a cooking-stove, lockers, bookshelves, a bird-cage with a canary in it, pots, pans, jugs, kettles——

Toad Ginger biscuits, potted lobster, sardines, gentleman's relish, bacon, cards, dominoes—an enormous trifle Cook prepared this morning—I thought we might tuck into that when we make our first stop this afternoon——

Rat Just a minute! Hold on! "Everything that *we* could possibly need"? "First stop this afternoon"?

Toad and Mole come out of the caravan

Toad Now, Ratty. Don't start getting stiff and sniffy—you know you've got to come.

Rat Oh, but I haven't. You always think that everyone has to do everything you say, Toady—but not me—not this time.

Mole Oh, can't we, Ratty?

Rat Certainly not.

Mole *Please*, Ratty.

Toad My dear, good, kind, agreeable Ratty, you've simply *got* to come, because I can't possibly manage without you. So please don't argue. You surely don't mean to stick to your dull, fusty old river all your life? I want to show you the world!

Rat I don't give an owl's hoot what you want, Toad. I'm not coming—and that's flat. And I *am* going to stick to my old river, *and* live in a hole. What's more, Mole's going to stick by me and do as I do, aren't you, Moley?

Mole I'll always stick by you, Ratty—what's a friend for? All the same, it does sound as if it might have been—well, what's the word?

Toad Adventureful?

Mole No...

Toad Excitingest and wondermost?

Mole No...

Toad Absolutelest unprecedentedly fantabulous?

Mole No ... oooh—not that either. Oh, bother—oh my—what *is* the word... I know! *Fun*. As if it might have been fun.

Toad I couldn't have chosen a better word myself, Moley. It *will* be fun. Such fun. Or it could have been, if only... Still—if Ratty's made his mind up, there's nothing more to be said. I'll just have to enjoy it on my own, that's all. Looking on the positive side: three times as much cream trifle.

Rat (*looking at the downcast Mole*) Oh, all right. Very well. We'll go.

Mole Hooray!

Rat But not because I approve of it, because I don't. And not just for Mole's sake either. It's because of you, Toad. Because you're not to be trusted on your own—and without the two of us along, I don't dare to think what trouble you'd get into.

Toad Just you wait until you're on the open road, Ratty—you'll enjoy it all right. Absolutely, unprecedentedly fantabulous!

Mole And, best of all, Ratty, it'll be *such* fun!

Mole
Rat (*singing*)

We have only just discovered
We are travelling men,
And we won't be back,
Until we really can't say when.
There's the highway,
There's the heath,
There's the country lane,
There's the common,
There's the hedgerow,
Here we go again.

All

We are travelling men
And the world's out there,
Here today,
Gone tomorrow haven't got a care.
There's the blue sky up above,
There are fields below,
And a sun to shine down on us,
Wherever we go!

Mole How soon can we leave?

Toad Immediately, of course. This very instant.

Rat Aren't you forgetting something?

Toad (*puzzled, looking all around*) Am I? No? I don't think so? I'm positive I've covered every conceivable contingency.

Mole What have we forgotten, Ratty?

Rat That caravan is hardly likely to trundle along unaided. Shouldn't there be a horse?

Toad Not *a* horse, Ratty. *The* horse. And of course I hadn't forgotten. I've found us the finest, fastest, surest-footedest steed that was ever shod. A tried and trusted companion who's as eager to be on the road as we are ourselves. Watch this. (*He puts his fingers into his mouth and whistles*)

A grey Pantomime Horse gallops on to the stage, does a couple of tired circuits and comes to a halt

The Mole and the Water-Rat are unimpressed

Rat Finest?
Mole Fastest?
Rat Surest-footedest my left whiskers!
Mole What's his name?
Toad Black Beauty.
Rat *Black* Beauty?
Mole But he's *grey*?
Toad Sshh! Don't let him hear you say that. *We* know he's grey. But *he* thinks he's black. He's jet-black and he's beautiful, aren't you, old fellow. What's more important, he's eager to carry us far o'er hill and dale, isn't that a fact?

The Pantomime Horse shakes its head

There you are—he said "yes".
Rat No, he didn't—he shook his head.
Toad Nodded, Ratty—he nodded "yes".

The Pantomime Horse continues to shake its head, forcefully, but Toad ignores this fact

Now, if you two chaps will be so kind as to give me a hand to get him between the shafts, we'll soon be on our way.

The three cluster round the Pantomime Horse which takes one look at the caravan and then gallops off around the stage. Rat, Mole and Toad pursue and recapture the Horse then, with a great deal of confusion, succeed in backing it between the shafts, with Toad bellowing orders

This way! To me! From you! Fasten that strap, Ratty! Do up that buckle, Mole, there's a useful chap. Nearly done. Now we have it. Lead him away, Ratty!

Rat takes hold of the bridle and leads the Pantomime Horse forward, leaving the caravan behind—we see that it is Toad himself and not the Horse, who is securely fastened in the shafts

No, no, no! You've got it wrong. Back him up again! Back, back, back! Steady … steady … steady…!

Mole and Rat back the Pantomime Horse into the shafts again. This time they succeed in both releasing Toad from the harness and replacing him with the Pantomime Horse

That's more like it! Now it's us for the open road!

They move off, circling the stage, singing. As they sing, day turns to night and the stars come out

All (*singing*)

La-la-la-la-la
La-la-la-la
La-la-la
La-la-la-la-la-la-la-la-la.
There's the blue sky up above,
There are fields below,
And a sun to shine upon us,
Wherever we go!

As the Pantomime Horse, the caravan and the three Travellers come to a halt, a campfire glows in the darkness. They sit around the campfire and sing in a slower tempo

We are travelling men,
And we've journeyed far,
First the day,
Then the darkness following our star.
There's the night-sky up above,
There is peace below,
And the countryside's our pillow,
Off to sleep we go.

Toad, Rat and Mole stretch out on the ground

Toad (*yawning*) This is the life for a gentleman, eh, Ratty? Talk about your old river!

Rat I don't talk about my river. You know I don't, Toad. But I *think* about it.

Mole It's no good, Ratty. He's not listening. He's fast asleep.

And, as if to prove Mole's point, Toad begins to snore softly but regularly

Rat I do think about the river, Moley—all the time.

The Mole reaches out for Rat's paw and gives it a gentle squeeze

Mole Have you had enough of caravanning, Ratty? Shall we run away tomorrow morning, quite early—very early—and go back to our dear old home on the river?

Rat No—we'll see it out. I said I'd stick by Toad—and I will. Until this trip is ended. It won't last very long. Toad's fads never do. Good-night, Moley.
Mole Good-night, Rat. Sleep well.
Mole
Rat } (*singing*) There's the night-sky up above,
There is peace below,
And the countryside's our pillow,
Off to sleep we go…

And, as the two friends join Toad in slumber, we fade to total darkness

Scene 3

The Open Road

The Lights come up again on the same scene at early morning. There is the sound of birdsong

Toad is harnessing the Pantomime Horse into the shafts as Mole and Rat waken and stretch themselves

Toad Come on, you lazybones! The sun and myself have both been up for hours. It's high time we were on the road again.
Rat What about breakfast?
Toad All in hand. Once we've got a few miles under our belts, we'll call a halt. You're in charge of breakfasts, Ratty: two boiled eggs, not *too* runny, and toasted soldiers. And you can serve them to me, Moley: silver teaspoon, clean napkin, neatly folded—oh, and you might just keep your eyes skinned for wild flowers—a few buttercups in a small jar would set my breakfast tray off nicely.

The Rat and the Mole exchange a horrified glance

During the following, Toad "clicks" his tongue at the Pantomime Horse and leads it quietly away, pulling the caravan

Rat Two boiled eggs? Toasted soldiers?
Mole Serve him his breakfast? With buttercups!

They turn their indignation towards Toad—who is no longer there. Over the following, we hear the sound of a fast-approaching car, accompanied by the "poop-pooping" of its horn

Rat Wait a minute, Toady!

Mole Toad, be careful of that motor-car!
Rat Toad… Look out!

The sound of a crash

The Pantomime Horse enters, minus the caravan, and circuits the stage, pursued by Mole

(*Calling into the distance*) Villains! Scoundrels! Highwaymen…! You… You roadhogs! I'll have the law on you! I'll drag you through every court in the land—see if I don't!

Mole's efforts to catch the Pantomime Horse fail and it gallops away

Toad enters, dazed but blissful, his hands grasping an imaginary steering-wheel

Toad Poop-poop! Poop-poop!
Rat It's all right, Toady. You're safe now. Pull yourself together, old chum.
Toad Poop-poop! Poop-poop!
Mole What is it, Toad? Are you all right?
Toad Poop-poop! Glorious stirring sight! The poetry of motion! The real way to travel. The *only* way to travel. Here today—the middle of next week tomorrow. Villages skipped through, towns and cities flashing by—here comes the next horizon. Oh, bliss! Oh, poop-poop! Oh joy! Oh me! Oh…

Song 4: Poop-Poop!

(*Singing*) Poop, poop,
Poop-poop,
There is magic in the air,
Poop, poop,
Poop-poop,
Close your eyes, you'll hear it everywhere,
Poop, poop,
Poop-poop,
All together shout "Hurrah!"
What have I seen,
Has my life been,
Unnecessary so far?
Such times I've missed,
Did time exist,
Before the motor car?

Mole Are you sure you're feeling all right, Toady?

Rat All right? He's completely out of his tiny green skull.

Toad (*singing*)
I just know,
That I must buy one,
I've got to sit behind the wheel of my own bus.
Don't tell me "No",
Don't scupper my fun,
Don't moan and groan,
Or shake your head,
And make a fuss,
But just go:

Poop, poop,
Poop-poop,
There is magic in the sound,
Poop, poop,
Poop-poop,
Even Mole could hear it underground,
Poop, poop,
Poop-poop,
All together shout "Hurrah!"
Old Toady's found it,
Stand and sound it,
A drum-roll ra-ta-ta-ta!
Such times I've missed,
Did time exist,
Before the motor car?

Rat Now see here, Toad—as soon as we get to the nearest village, Moley and I will find a blacksmith and arrange for the caravan to be fetched and mended and put to rights. You, meanwhile, will seek out the local constable. He can find out who that car belongs to, and you must lodge a complaint against the owner… Toad? Toad! Have you heard one single word I've said?

Toad Police station? Complain? About that beautiful wonderful vehicle? Have the caravan mended? I've done with caravans forever. I never want to see or hear of caravans again. Poop-poop!

Rat (*to Mole*) It's hopeless.

Mole Toady—do see sense.

Rat I recognize that face he's wearing. He won't see sense of his own accord, Moley. It's our job to teach him some.

Mole / **Rat** (*singing*)
We just know,
That it's the wrong road,
He is travelling the one that leads to doom.

Can't let him go,
Don't be an ass, Toad,
But what's the use?
No matter how
We rant and fume,
He'll just go:

Toad Poop, poop,
Poop-poop,

Mole
Rat He's as mad as a march hare.

Toad Poop, poop,
Poop-poop,

Mole
Rat All pedestrians should have a care.

Toad Poop, poop,
Poop-poop,

All All together shout "Hurrah!"
What have [has] I [he] seen,
Has my [his] life been,
Unnecessary so far?
Such times I've [he's] missed,
Did time exist,
Before that motor car!

And, at the end of the number, Rat and Mole watch horrified

Toad exits in his imaginary vehicle, still chanting "Poop-poop"

Mole What are we going to do about him, Ratty?
Rat Nothing——
Mole —But, Ratty——
Rat —for the sole and simple reason that there's nothing to *be* done. I know him of old. Toad is now possessed. He's besotted by a new craze.
Mole But what's to become of him?
Rat Oh, Toad's all right. He always is. He'll poop-poop along, on his merry way, in his imaginary motor car until someone out there is fool enough to sell him a real motor vehicle—and then look out!
Mole Isn't there anyone who might *talk* some sense into him?
Rat Badger might, I suppose—but he's the only one.
Mole Well then—let's go and get Badger.
Rat Quite out of the question. He lives in the very middle of the Wild Wood. And who wants to go there?

A musical chord, struck after each of the following three sentences, reminds us of the threat of the Wild Wood. Rat nods in answer to all three questions

Mole Because of the weasels? And foxes? And stoats?

Rat glances up at the sky

Rat Particularly at this time of year, with winter not far away. Oh, bother Toad. Happily for you and I, Moley, Toad's probably miles away from here by now——

Mole (*interrupting*) He isn't, Ratty!

Toad enters at speed and still driving his make-believe motor car. He has managed to acquire some motoring gear: an overcoat, a cap, a pair of goggles and a scarf

Mole and Rat watch, as if transfixed, as Toad circuits the stage and then bears down on them

Toad Poop-poop! Poop-poop!

Toad exits, with Mole and Rat in hot pursuit

Rat Come back! Come back!

Toad's "Poop-poops" fade off into the distance as the Lights fade

Scene 4

The Wild Wood

It is dusk on a winter's afternoon—there are patches of snow

Mole (*off*) Badger? Badger!

Mole enters, glancing anxiously over his shoulder, but never quite managing to catch sight of the quick, darting heads of the Weasels, Stoats and Foxes that comprise the Wild-Wooders and who are following Mole's progress through the trees. Mole, aware of something or someone at his back, turns quickly—but again too late

Badger? Badger, is that you? Bad-ger…!

Mole's nervous cry is mimicked, tauntingly, by a Wild-Wooder

Wild-Wooder Bad-ger…

Mole Ratty, is that you? No, of course it isn't. You'd *never* play those kind of tricks on me. Oh, I do wish that I hadn't come here on my own. The main thing is not to be afraid of shadows—particularly my own. P'raps if I whistled—that might keep my spirits up?

He whistles a few nervous notes which are echoed mockingly by another of the Wild-Wooders—and then another—and then more

Who's that? Who is it? Who's there?

We go into a number in which the Wild-Wooders tease and torment Mole as he continues through the wood, finally spinning him across the stage and causing him to trip and fall

Song 5: Beware!

Wild-Wooders Beware,
Take care where you tread your feet,
Because of the ones you dread to meet,
They're out tonight,
To give you a fright.
Despair,
Watch out where you steer your hand,
Look out for the fearful band,
Whatever you do.
'Cos following close behind you is,
This villainous crew.

When it grows dark,
And starts getting colder,
Look over your shoulder,
There's nobody there.
As night-time grows
A little bit older,
We start getting bolder,
You'll get such a scare.

Take heed,
You'll need to feel your way,
Before ever your hair turns grey,
You'll kneel and pray,

And wish that we'd call it a day.
Concede,
We'll have you on your knees,
You'll shiver, begin to freeze,
Start uttering pleas,
And muttering "please, oh please,
Oh please,
Go away".

Between the trees,
We'll come out to find you,
So look out behind you,
There's nobody there.
Where no-one sees,
We'll reach out and touch you,
And just think how much you'll
Get one heck of a scare.

Take heed,
You'll need to feel your way,
Before ever your hair turns grey,
You'll kneel and pray,
And wish that we'd call it a day.
Concede,
We'll have you on your knees,
You'll shiver, begin to freeze,
Start uttering pleas
And muttering "please, oh please,
Oh please,
Go away.
Oh please,
Go away!"

The Wild-Wooders circle the fallen Mole, taunting him, and he cowers in a hollow, shaking with fear

Mole Oh please, oh please, oh *please*—go away!

The Wild-Wooders disappear

Mole, hiding his head in his hands, is unaware that they have gone

Rat (*off*) Moley!

Rat enters, armed to the teeth—and we realize why the Wild-Wooders left in such a hurry. He has a brace of pistols tucked in at his belt and he is carrying a stout cudgel

Moley? Where are you? It's me—it's old Rat! Moh-ley…!

Mole takes his hands from his ears, opens his eyes, and peers out from his hiding place

Mole Ratty? Is it really you?

Rat There you are—thank goodness! You shouldn't have come here alone, Mole. I did warn you about the Wild Wood.

Mole I wanted to find Badger.

Rat Far easier said than done. Badger is the best of fellows—except you must not only take him *as* you find him—but *when* you find him.

Mole I wanted to talk to him about Toad.

Rat Then you should have talked to me first, Mole. And I would have talked you out of it. We river-bankers never come here by ourselves. If we do have to come, we come in twos—if not in pairs—then we're generally all right. (*He looks around and shivers*) We can't spend the night here—too cold for one thing.

Mole Dear Ratty, I'm most awfully sorry, but I can't go another step. And I've hurt my shin where I tripped and fell.

Rat Poor old Moley. This hasn't been your day. Let me see.

The Mole bares his leg and Rat examines the wound

You have been in the wars, old chap. You've cut it sure enough. Wait till I get at my handkerchief and I'll tie it up for you.

Mole (*miserably*) I must have tripped over a tree stump or a fallen branch. Oh, my! Oh my!

The Rat has produced a red spotted handkerchief and now proceeds to bind up the wound

Rat It's a very clean cut—that can't have been done by a tree stump or a branch.

Mole Well, never mind what done it. It hurts just the same, whatever done it.

Rat No—it was done by something straight and sharp. Hang on a minute, Moley. (*He starts to burrow in the snow*)

Mole rises, glances around, impatient and again fearful

Mole Oh, do come along, Rat! It was you that said we had to get away. It's getting darker by the second. This is no time to be making snowmoles.

Rat Hooray! (*He has uncovered a door-scraper and he gets to his feet and does a little jig of joy*) Hooray-oo-ray-oo-ray-oo-ray-oo-ray-oo-jolly-well-ray!

Mole What is it?

Rat Come and take a look!

As the Rat continues his little dance, the Mole hobbles back and examines the door-scraper

Mole (*unimpressed*) It's a door-scraper.

Rat Yes!

Mole I've seen plenty of those before—lots of times. Scores of them. I don't see that a door-scraper's worth making a song and dance about.

Rat But don't you see what it means, you—you dull-witted Moley?

Mole Of course I do. It means that some *extremely* careless and forgetful person has left his door-scraper lying about in the middle of the Wild Wood—*just* where it's *sure* to trip up some poor person. Very thoughtless of him, I call it. But I still don't see what there is to make a fuss over.

Rat Oh dear, oh dear! Here, do stop chattering and come and scrape.

But the Mole declines and it is Rat again who sets the snow flying as he burrows deeper and uncovers something else

There! What did I tell you?

Mole (*even more unimpressed*) It's a doormat.

Rat Yes! Isn't it wonderful?

Mole Wonderful? Because you've found another item of domestic litter? Go on then. Get it over with. Dance your little jig around it and then, perhaps, we can be on our way. *Wonderful*? A doormat? Can we *eat* a doormat? Or sleep under a doormat? Or sit on a doormat and sledge home over the snow on it, you exasperating rodent?

Rat Do—you—mean—to—say—that this doormat doesn't *tell* you anything?

Mole Not a sausage. Really, Rat, whoever heard of a doormat *telling* anyone anything? They simply don't go in for it. Doormats know their place. They get trodden on.

Rat Now, look here, you thick-headed animal... No, wait a minute—watch this—(*he burrows again at the snow and this time uncovers a dark-green door with an iron bell-pull hung by the side of an inscribed brass plate*)—and read that.

Mole "Mr Badger"! Ratty, you're a wonder! I see it all now. You argued it out, step by step, in that wise head of yours, from the very moment that I fell and cut my shin. You looked at the cut and, right away, your majestic mind said to itself… "Door-scraper!" And did you stop there? Not likely! Some people would have been quite satisfied, but not you. Your magnificent intellect went on working. "Let me only just find a doormat," says you to yourself, "and I'll show you a front door!" If only I had your head, Ratty, I could——

Rat silences Mole by tugging at the bell-pull which produces a jangling sound a long way off

The door opens slightly and Badger peers out

Badger Now, see here—the very next time this happens, I shall be exceedingly angry. Who is it this time, disturbing folk on such a night? Speak up?

Rat It's me, Badger. Rat—and my friend Mole.

A light is switched on over the green door, casting a warm glow

Badger (*stepping out*) What, Ratty, my dear little man! Well I never! And Mole too. What are you pair doing in the Wild Wood? At this hour?

Rat I came to look for Mole who'd set out to look for you.

Badger Alone?

Mole It was urgent. I wanted to talk to you about Mr Toad.

Badger Toady? Oh dear! What's he been up to this time?

Rat Going from bad to worse mainly. He will keep on buying motor car after motor car.

Mole And smashing them.

Badger How many has he had so far?

Rat Motor cars or smashes? Not that it makes any difference—it's the same thing with Toad. He's hopeless in a car. Badger, oughtn't we to *do* something?

Badger looks from Rat to Mole then back again—and arrives at a momentous decision

Badger You're right. The hour has come.

Mole What hour is that, Badger?

Badger Why, Toad's hour, of course! The hour of Toad!

Rat Hooray! We'll teach him to be a sensible Toad!

Badger We'll take him in hand.

Mole Is that the right thing to do?

Badger It's the *only* thing…

Song 6: Taken In Hand

(*Singing*)	He's got to be taken in hand,
Mole / **Rat**	In hand?
Badger	It's high time someone made a stand,
Mole / **Rat**	A stand?
Badger	It's the end of the road, Irresponsible Toad, He's got to be taken in hand.
Mole / **Rat**	That's grand.
Badger	For this time he's gone far too far,
Mole / **Rat**	Too far?
Badger	He's smashed up his last motor car,
Mole / **Rat**	Last car?
Badger	The point has to be made, When the piper's been paid, That this time he's gone far too far,
Mole / **Rat**	Hurrah!
Badger	When a fellow's bad behaviour is a burden to his chums, When his actions show no reasons or no rhymes, You may take it as a certain fact the hour surely comes, When he's made to stand and answer for his crimes,
Mole / **Rat**	Every time!
Badger	An amphibian's accountable like him or me or you, For his social class I couldn't give a hoot, He is not above the law because he's got a bob or two, Be he frog or be he toad or be he newt,
Mole / **Rat**	How astute!
Badger	We're doing it for his own good,
Mole / **Rat**	Own good?
Badger	He'd do it for us if he could,
Mole / **Rat**	He would?
Badger	We are not interfering by guiding and steering, We'll make Toad behave as he should,

Mole | **Rat** Understood!
Badger We'll stand up and lay down the law,
Mole | **Rat** The law,
Badger And give him a bit of what for!
Mole | **Rat** What for?
Badger It is time he was rueing,
His awful misdoing,
If not—then we'll give him some more,
Mole | **Rat** That's for sure!
Badger When a chap you've known for ages starts behaving like a cad,
When his lifestyle is a singular disgrace,
You don't sit back and ponder on the good times that you had,
You go straight round there and tell him to his face,
Mole | **Rat** At a pace!
Badger To be there in times of trouble, that is what a chum's about,
When a comrade's in default you're on parade,
With a shoulder he can lean on or to add a bit of clout,
For with friends like us the fellow's got it made,
Mole | **Rat** We're top grade!

Rat When do we start?

Badger You two animals will accompany me instantly to Toad Hall and the rescue work will be immediately undertaken.

Rat We'll rescue the poor unhappy creature, Badger—we'll convert him.

Badger He'll be the most converted Toad that ever was when we've done with him.

Mole (*tentatively*) Won't it wait until after Christmas?

Badger | **Rat** (*together*) Certainly not! We'll start at once.

Badger If not sooner!

All (*singing*) With a shoulder he can lean on or to add a bit of clout
For with friends like us the fellow's got it made!
For we're top grade.

The Lights fade

Scene 5

Outside Toad Hall

Which need consist of no more than an ornate front door with an impressive brass door-knocker

A number of Fieldmice, all with red mufflers round their necks, and with one of them carrying a lantern, are standing outside. Their spokesman, the 1st Fieldmouse, approaches the front door, rather nervously, and raps the door-knocker

The door is opened by Enid, the housemaid, who beams down at the diminutive Fieldmice

Enid Aw…
1st Mouse We're carol-singers. We're carol-singing.
Enid I'm Enid. I'm the housemaid. Well—learning to be. I'll nip up to the attic for my purse. You lot sing up—I'll leave the door open.

Enid scoots off

The Fieldmice take up their choral positions

1st Mouse Clear your throats—stand up straight—wipe your nose, Maisie—what shall we give her?
2nd Mouse (*impishly*) While shepherds washed their dirty socks.
1st Mouse Belt up, Melvyn.

But the 2nd Fieldmouse's witticism has occasioned a fit of giggling from the other Fieldmice and he is encouraged to try again

2nd Mouse Good King Wenceslas,
Knocked a bobby senseless,
Right in the middle of Marks & Spencer's——

1st Mouse (*sternly*) If you don't belt up, Melvyn, this minute, you're going straight home and you won't come carol-singing again. It's *Rejoice, Rejoice*—no coughing—after I say "One, two, three". One, two, three…

By the light of the moon, supplemented by the orange glow from the upheld lantern, the Fieldmice raise their voices and sing to the open door

Song 7: Rejoice, Rejoice

All Rejoice, rejoice, all Christian men,
For Christ Our Lord is born again,
Laid inside a stable far,
Nestling down beneath the star,
Christ is born again,
Christ is born again.
Sing out, sing loud, all of mankind,
For Jesus Christ the infant child,
Came to earth from heaven above,
Son of God and bearing love,
Christ is born again,
Christ is born again.

There are several moments of silence, as the Fieldmice stand respectfully outside the open door

3rd Mouse She's coming!

It is not Enid who appears however, but Hawkins, the butler, in full butlering costume and carrying a bright yellow duster

Hawkins 'Oppit, you lot. Go on, vamoose! Skedaddle!
2nd Mouse We've just sung a carol.
Hawkins H'I knows you 'ave. H'I could 'ear your caterwauling below stairs in the pantry. Which one of you knocked on that door-knocker?
1st Mouse I did.
Hawkins Don't do it again then. Look at it! Covered in fingermarks. You ought to be downright ashamed of yourselves, the lot of you... Buzz off! Didn't you 'ear me the first time?
1st Mouse But Enid said——
Hawkins H'Enid? H'Enid! 'Oo's h'Enid, when she's at 'ome? H'I'll tell you 'oo h'Enid is—she's a h'employee—that's h'Enid's lot in life. H'and h'employees don't h'engage carol-singers! No, and they don't leave the front door wide h'open neither! You might h'easily have woke up the master—'ee's got a h'early start tomorrer, 'as Mr Toad. There's a shiny, spanking brand new motor car what's being delivered in the morning. That's h'all 'ee needs tonight, innit? A pack of Fieldmice, causing disruptions and finger-marking 'is door-knocker. Go on—buzz off!
1st Mouse But——
Hawkins "But", "but", "but"—don't you "but" me, or you'll feel the toe-end of my boot! Go on—last time of telling: 'op it!

The Fieldmice sigh and trudge off dispiritedly, as Hawkins goes back to polishing the door-knocker. The 2nd Fieldmouse takes advantage of Hawkins's turned back to blow him a raspberry. Hawkins wheels, angrily

Get aht of it, you 'orrible little 'ooligans—afore I sets the ginger cat on yer!

The Fieldmice take to their heels

Hawkins shakes out his duster and goes indoors

A moment later, Enid returns, clutching her purse

Enid Found it at last—and there's a bright new sixpence here that—Oh! They've gone—Aw ... what a pity...
Hawkins (*off*) H'Enid? H'Eee-nid...!
Enid Coming, Mr Hawkins!

The door closes behind Enid as the Lights fade to black—then up to morning

Hawkins comes out with a couple of empty milk bottles which he sets down outside the front door

Rat and Mole arrive on the scene

Rat Good-morning! Is Mr Toad at home?
Hawkins (*surveying the visitors sourly*) No, 'ee ain't. And 'ee ain't likely to be at 'ome neither. 'Oo shall I tell 'im 'ee ain't in to?
Rat Ratty.
Mole Mole.

Badger who has been strolling along behind the other two, arrives, swishing a stout stick

Badger And Badger.
Hawkins Oh! Oh well, that's different then. 'Ee might very well be in—I'll 'ave to check on it. (*He opens the door*) Cor blimey, 'ow's that for a coincidence? 'Ere 'ee is!

Toad sweeps out, cigar in hand, and got up in his motoring finery

Toad Ratty! Mole! Badger! You couldn't have arrived at a more opportune moment!

Badger exchanges meaningful glances with his two companions and replies ominously

Badger So it would seem, Toad.
Toad Has the new car been delivered, 'Awkins? (*Correcting himself*) Hawkins?
Hawkins It 'as h'indeed, sir. And it ain't 'arf a spanker! I'm 'aving it got ready for you now. H'Enid, the new 'ousemaid's h'attending to its 'ead-lamps; Bertram the boot-boy's beavering away, buffing up the bumpers and the boot, while Garside the gardener's going great guns grafting on the gear-box with the grease-gun.
Toad Good grief—that's grand! (*To his visitors*) It's the very latest model. It's a yellow one. As soon as it's ready we can all go for a jolly—go for a jolly—er, you know...

As the trio bear down on him, Toad tootles an imaginary horn, hesitantly

Poop-Poop?
Badger Mr Toad has had a change of plan. He won't be requiring the new car today. He won't be requiring your services either—off you go.
Hawkins (*looking doubtfully at Toad*) Shall I polish the silver, sir?
Badger You can polish your head for all I care, fellow! Scoot!

Hawkins beats a hasty retreat

Badger, Rat and Mole advance again on Toad

Toad What's all this about, you chaps? What's to do?
Badger You'll find out. First of all, you can take off those ridiculous garments.
Toad Shan't! This is a gross outrage. I demand an instant explanation.
Badger Very well, Toad—if you won't do it for yourself, we shall have to do it for you. See to it, you two.

Rat and Mole take hold of the reluctant Toad. During the following they succeed in divesting Toad of his motoring gear

Toad Get back! Hands off! Don't you dare lay a paw on me—either of you! I'm Toad! Intelligent Toad! Clever Toad! Toad the Terror of the Road! Toad the Maestro of the motor car! No, Ratty! Stop it, Mole! I say, chaps, no... *Please*! ... (*Etc.*)

Toad's bluster appears to evaporate with the removal of his outer clothing—

which now lies scattered around the drive. He giggles, feebly, and looks appealingly at each of his friends in turn

Badger (*severely*) You knew it must come to this, sooner or later, Toad. You've disregarded all of the warnings we've given you. You're getting us animals a bad name in the district by your furious driving and your smashes and your rows with the police. Now, you're a good fellow at heart and I don't want to be too hard on you. I'm taking you back indoors, Toad, and I'm going to give you a good long talking-to—and we'll see what that does for you.

Toad No, Badger, *please*, Badger—not one of your dressing-downs. Anything but that.

Badger
Rat
Mole } We're behaving as all best friends would

Toad Sez you!

Badger
Rat
Mole } You'd do it for us if you could

Toad Sez who!

Badger
Rat
Mole }
You'll laud us, applaud us
Find ways to reward us
We're doing it for your own good
So we should!

The Lights fade

Scene 6

Toad's Bedroom

A spacious room furnished in four-poster elegance. There is a door leading to a dressing-room and another door leading to the landing and stairs. There is a mullioned window in the rear wall

Rat and Mole are sitting in comfy chairs: Rat is lounging at his ease while Mole is plainly on edge. With them, from behind the closed door of the dressing-room, we can hear the continuous drone of Badger's voice, rising and falling in waves of oratory as he lectures Toad

Badger (*off*) Are you listening to me, Toad?

Mole How long has he had him in there now?

Rat (*consulting his pocket-watch*) Forty-three minutes, by my reckoning.

Mole Forty-three minutes without even once stopping for breath! Poor old Toady! (*He gets to his feet, crosses and opens the dressing-room door a couple of inches, gently*)

We can now hear Badger's voice clearly

Badger (*off*) ...which, believe you me, Toad, is certainly no more nor less than you deserve. You should be bally-well ashamed of yourself—and if you aren't now, then you jolly well ought to be! And *another* thing, and I've been intending to take this up with you for longer than I care to think...

Mole has gently closed the door

Mole He certainly knows how to dish out a ticking off.

Song 8: Talking to Toad

(*Singing*) He's giving him a fearful earful,
He's tearing off a frightful strip.
Poor old Toad, he's nearly tearful,
Good old Badger's letting rip!

Rat, who has got to his feet and is standing with his hands behind his back in front of the fireplace, shrugs laconically and sings, à la Noël Coward

Rat That won't cure him...
(*Singing*) Talking to Toad
Is a terrible waste of time,
Try appealing to Toad,
It's not worth a fig or a dime.
You can threaten,
You can bluster,
He'll say anything that suits,
And for all the threats you muster,
Toady doesn't give two hoots.

Mole gently opens the dressing-room door and, again, we hear Badger's voice

Badger (*off*) I sometimes wonder, Toad, what's to become of you? I sometimes wonder if you even know yourself? And, another thing...

Mole has again closed the dressing-room door

Mole He's bawling Toad out something shocking,
He's handing him a dressing-down,
Poor old Toad, his knees are knocking,
Badger's really going to town!

Rat (*yawning*) I keep telling you, Mole:
(*Singing*) Ticking off Toad,
You might as well not begin,
Shoot a rocket at Toad,
The bounder will stand there and grin.
You can rant and
You can thunder,
You can stand and shake your fist,
At the end you'll only wonder,
Has Toad even got the gist?

Pleading with Toad,
Even pulling out all the stops,
I've a feeling that Toady's
The one that'll come out tops.
You can argue,
You can reason,
Toad'll give you tit-for-tat,
But for all the good that you do—
You might as well talk to the cat!

The door to the dressing-room opens and Badger thrusts a limp and dejected Toad into the bedroom

Badger And that's that!

Mole gives Rat an "I-told-you-so" look as Badger points to a chair

Sit down there, Toad. My friends, I am happy to report a one hundred per cent success. Toad has seen the error of his ways. He is truly sorry for his misguided conduct in the past, and he has undertaken to give up motor cars entirely. I have his solemn promise to that effect.

Mole That's wonderful news!

Rat (*giving Toad a long, hard, searching look*) Wonderful news indeed, if only ... if only...

Badger (*unaware of Rat's misgivings*) There's only one more thing to be done. Toady, I want you solemnly to repeat, in front of your friends here, exactly what you admitted to me in that dressing-room just now? First, that you're sorry for what you've done—and that you now see the folly of it all.

There is a pause, during which Toad looks, desperately, this way and that and then, finally

Toad No!
Badger No?
Toad No, I'm not sorry! Not one little bit. And it wasn't folly at all! It was simply glorious!
Badger What? You deceitful back-sliding amphibian, didn't you promise just now, in there——
Toad Oh yes, yes, in *there*! I'd have said anything in *there*. You're so eloquent, dear Badger, and so moving, and so convincing, and you put all your points so frightfully well—you can do what you like with me in there. But out *here* it's an entirely different kettle of tadpoles! If you want the truth, Badger, I'm not a bit sorry or repentant really—so it's no earthly good now me saying I am, is it?
Badger Do you mean to say that you don't promise never to touch a motor car again?
Toad Certainly not. On the contrary, I faithfully promise that the very first motor car I see, off I go in it! The very first. If I have to beg, borrow or even *steal* it. Poop-poop.
Badger Did you say "Poop-poop"? To *me*?
Toad I did—and I'll say it again—two times: Poop-poop! Poop-poop!
Rat (*to Mole*) There? What did I tell you?
(*Singing*) Ticking off Toad,
Is a game that you just cannot win,
At the end of the road,
Toad gives not a rusty old pin.
Badger's ranted
Badger's bullied
Badger's been on his high horse,
Badger Now it's over,
Was it worth it?
All Three All Toad understands is force!
Toad Invincible Toad! (*He leaps to his feet and thrusts a victorious fist into the air*)

The Lights fade

Scene 7

The same. Several days later

Mole is alone in the bedroom, yawning and stretching

Badger enters with Rat. They have towels round their necks and have just completed their morning toilet

Badger (*glancing anxiously around*) Where's Toad?
Mole (*jerking his head towards the dressing-room*) Getting dressed.
Rat How is he this morning?
Mole Just the same. I can't get much out of him. Except, "Oh, leave me alone", and "It may pass off in time", and so on. Are you sure we're doing the right thing, Badger? We've been taking it in turns to guard him for a week now—and Toad hasn't changed at all.
Badger I said at the start that it wouldn't be easy—that it would take patience.
Rat It's for Toady's own good, Mole. Think what fun we'll all have when he's himself again.
Badger But until that day dawns, he mustn't be left alone for a single second—not until the poison's out of his system. Your turn for sentry-go this morning, Ratty. I'm off to stretch my legs. How about you, Mole? Fancy a lope around the woods before breakfast?
Mole Rather, Badger!

They cross to the door, where Badger pauses

Badger Now you look out, Rat. If Toad's quiet and polite and behaving like the recipient of a Sunday School prize—then he's only being artful. Mark my words, he's up to something.
Rat He won't put anything over on me, Badger. Don't worry—have a good time, you two.

Badger and Mole exit

A moment later, Toad enters from the dressing-room in his night-shirt, shoulders drooping and apparently low in spirit

Toady? I thought you were getting dressed?

Toad clambers dejectedly into bed, then pulls the bed-clothes up around him

What is it, old chap? Aren't you feeling well?
Toad (*feebly*) Thank you so much, dear Ratty. So good of you to enquire. But, first of all, tell me how you are yourself? And the excellent Mole, bless him? And the stout-hearted Badger?
Rat Oh, *we're* all right. It's such a grand morning. Why don't you make the effort, Toady? Come on—jump up out of bed, eh? Put some clothes on?
Toad Jump? Oh dear, kind Rat, how little you realize my condition. And how very far I am from "jumping up" now—if ever again.

Rat What is it, Toad? What's wrong with you? Is there anything I can do?

Toad Don't trouble yourself on my account, Ratty. I do so hate being a burden—but I'm sure I won't be a bother to you much longer.

Rat Well, I hope not too. And I'm glad to hear that it's going to stop. What with the weather being so glorious and the boating season just beginning. It isn't the bother that we mind—but you are making us miss such a lot.

Toad No, it *is* the trouble I'm causing. I can quite understand how you feel. You're tired of having to put up with me. I'm a nuisance, I know I am.

Rat Nothing of the kind, Toady. We're your *friends*. Gosh, Toady, if you can't count on us, who can you count on?

Song 9: What's a Friend For

(*Singing*) What's a friend for?
To see the night through,
Lend you a paw,
Make trouble light, too.
Why have a chum,
If he's not there,
When there is thunder?
When rain clouds form,
Before a storm,
He'll find a spot you both can
Shelter under.

What's a friend for?
To have some fun with,
Meadow or shore,
Run in the sun with,
Chase clouds away
Enjoy today,
Go find a rainbow,
You and your friend
Will sit and wonder where did
All that rain go?

What's friendship for
If not for sharing,
Without a flaw,
Loving and caring.
What is a friend,
A friend like Mole,
He's half of me,
He makes me whole.

What's a friend for?
Someone to turn to,
Keep open his door,
When others spurn you,
Be star-shine bright,
Make darkness light,
Stay close to you tonight,
And evermore,
That's what friends are for.

So you see, Toady, we'd take any trouble on earth for you, if only you'd be a sensible amphibian.

Toad (*weakly*) If I thought that, Ratty, then I would beg you to step round to the village as fast as you can and fetch the doctor.

Rat The doctor?

Toad No, no—don't bother. It's probably too late for that—and I don't want to be a bother. We may as well let things take their course.

Rat What things? Which course? Why do you need a doctor?

Toad No matter… Tomorrow you'll probably be thinking, "Oh, if only I'd done something at the time." But you mustn't blame yourself, Ratty. I forgive you… Forget I ever asked.

Rat Look here, Toad—of course I'll get a doctor for you. But it's not *that* bad, surely? Can't it wait until Moley and Badger get back?

Toad Don't bother, don't bother. What could a doctor do anyway? I'm only grasping at straws. It'd probably be too late by the time he got here… (*He lets out a long, loud sigh and sinks back on to his pillow*)

Rat Toad? Toady? Listen, old fellow. I'll go and get the doctor at once. Can you hear me, Toad? Lie still, old chap, and try not to move. Hold on, Toad—be brave—I'll run there and back.

Rat exits

Toad sits up

Rat opens the door again for a final check

Toad instantly collapses

Rat exits again, locking the door behind him

Toad leaps out of bed

Toad Ingenious Toad! Sagacious Toad! Smart piece of work that! Brain against brute force—and brain came out on top. (*During the following he* *takes off his night-shirt to reveal that he is "under-dressed" in his motoring gear*)

(*Declaiming*) The world has held great heroes,
As history books have showed,
But never a name to go down to fame,
Compared with that of Toad!
Poop-Poop!

He produces his goggles and motoring cap from underneath the pillow. Throwing back the eiderdown, he reveals that he has previously knotted the sheets together, in preparation for his escape. He secures one end of his "sheet-rope" and throws the other end out of the window, as:

Poor old Ratty! Won't he catch it when Badger gets back? A worthy fellow, the Water-Rat, with many good qualities, but with very little intelligence—compared with the talented Toad, that is! Resourceful Toad! Inestimable Toad! Poop-poop! Poop-poop!

Toad effects his escape through the window as the Lights fade

Scene 8

The Village

Basically the bare stage

Badger, Mole and Rat enter in some concern, looking anxiously around

Mole Oh my! Oh, my Ratty! Oh my, oh my!

Badger Far be it for me to criticise—but you've certainly been a bit of a duffer this time, Ratty.

Rat He did it awfully well, Badger.

Badger He did you awfully well. Still, talking won't mend matters. And he can't have got very far—we ought to be able to find him before he gets himself into more hot water.

Mole Here comes the village constable. Let's ask him if he's seen Toad.

The rural Constable enters, intent on notebook and pencil

Badger Excuse us, officer—we're looking for a friend of ours. I don't suppose you've seen him, by any chance?

Constable Sorry, gentlemen, I'm unable to assist you at this moment. On account of the fact that I'm hot on the trail of an unmitigated villain—a public menace who must be apprehended at all costs.

Mole Who is it?

Rat What's he done?

Constable Taking your questions one at a time, at the present moment the miscreant's identity is unknown. Suffice it to say, investigations are ongoing. With regard to what he's done—I might very well reply: "What *hasn't* he done?" He's misappropriated a motor vehicle, he's driven the said motor vehicle without due care and attention and to the public danger, he's exceeded the speed limit, he's terrorised the public highway—you name the offence, gentlemen, and the rapscallion's committed it. As to his description, sir—well, there we do have a breakthrough. According to eyewitness accounts, and there are several, he's green all over.

Mole Green?

Rat All over?

Constable With big yellow spots. (*He gives an involuntary shiver*) Horrible, isn't it? Added to which, he has a curious habit which ought to make him stand out in a crowd. He goes "Poop-poop".

Mole Poop?

Rat Poop?

Badger Poop-poop?

Constable That's it, sirs! That's it exactly! It's as if you... This friend of yours? You never know, I might just chance across him while I'm looking for my bloke. Has your chum got any distinguishing marks or funny habits?

Mole None at all, Constable—forget him.

Rat It's not important.

Badger He's probably safe back home by now.

Constable Whatever you say—but I was just beginning to wonder...

Luckily, before the Constable can pursue his new train of thought, the Villagers arrive on the scene, highly excited

1st Villager Constable, Constable—there's a madman at large in the High Street!

2nd Villager He's driving a car along the pavement.

3rd Villager He's frightening the babies!

4th Villager He's terrifying old ladies!

5th Villager He's startling the horses!

6th Villager He's going "Poop-poop!"

Constable Poop-poop?

Song 10: Poop-Poop! (Reprise)

Villagers Poop-poop,
Poop-poop,
It's the only sound he knows.
Poop-poop,
Poop-poop,
You can hear it everywhere he goes.
Poop-poop,
Poop-poop,
Stand together, show him how,
When will it cease,
Is there no peace,
From this continual row.
Give him what for,
Lay down the law,
And apprehend him now!

Constable I'll have you know,
That I detest him,
And I intend to slip the handcuffs on that rogue,
"Hello, hello!"
When I arrest him,
To gaol he'll sail,
And in his cell,
In Toadish brogue
He'll just go…

Rat
Badger
Mole Poop-poop,
Poop-poop,
Old Toady's on the loose.
Poop-poop,
Poop-poop,
The foolish bounder's cooked his goose.
Poop-poop,
Poop-poop,
All together cry,

Mole Oh my!

Rat
Mole To save his skin,
He's hovering on the brink,
We're much too late,
Toad's sealed his fate,
He's headed straight for clink!

Company Poop-poop,
Poop-poop,

Poop-poop,
That Toad's gone far too far.
Poop-poop,
Poop-poop,
He's a menace in a motor car.
Poop-poop,
Poop-poop,
All together shout "Stop thief!"
Protect our road,
Secure that Toad,
The villain's flipped his brain.
Up goes the shout,
"Look out! Look out!"
For here he comes again!

The entire Company scatter as:

Toad drives on in an impressive car, roars across the stage and exits on the opposite side. A moment later we hear a horrendous crash

A single car wheel bounces on to the stage and rolls into the orchestra pit while the Constable takes feverish, copious notes

CURTAIN

ACT II

Scene 1

The Courtroom

With Toad's trial about to take place, there is an air of eager anticipation. The aged judge, Justice R. De Veering (whose eyesight and hearing could be better) is seated behind his desk in his imposing chair. The jury members, consisting entirely of Wild-Wooders, are seated in the jury-box. Also present in court are Badger, in wig and gown and representing Toad, and Rat and Mole who are there to testify as character witnesses on Toad's behalf. There is also a Clerk-of-Court who sits behind a tall desk and takes down the court's proceedings with a quill pen and a parchment document

As the chatter from the Wild-Wooders increases, the Judge raps for order with his gavel

Judge Order in court! Order in court!
Clerk Bring forth the accused!

The Constable ushers Toad up into the dock. Toad's appearance occasions hisses and boos from the jury members who have already made up their mind as to Toad's guilt

Judge Order in court! Order! Order!
Clerk This court is now in session, with his lordship, Justice R. De Veering, in attendance. Case Number One: The Crown versus Toad. (*He hands over to the Judge the documents appertaining to the case*)

The Constable has pushed Toad on to the seat in the dock—Toad is now barely visible to the court

Judge Is the accused here present?
Clerk He's in the dock, m'lud.
Judge Eh? Eh? What's that?
Clerk I said "He's in the dock, m'lud". "Dock! Dock!"
Judge Duck? D'yer say "Duck?" He's not going to start throwing things, is

he? Just because I'm going to send him to prison? (*To the Constable*) Because, if so, I'm warning you here and now, that you'll only make things worse for yourself! I shall deal very sharply with you, to put it bluntly! D'y'hear me?

Constable I'm the Constable, m'lud.

Judge What's he say? Speak up, man! Speak up!

Constable I said "I'm the Constable, m'lud". I've been sworn in! Constable!

Judge I don't care if you were born in Dunstable, or anywhere else for that matter.

Toad is now on his feet and the Judge sees him for the first time

Good gracious me, there are two of them! What's that one called?

Clerk That's Toad, m'lud! That's the accused.

The announcement is greeted with more boos and hisses from the Wild-Wooders

Judge Order, Order! (*He peers at Toad*) What do you reckon I should give him? Would five years be enough—or should I double it? What's he done exactly?

The Clerk refers to the documentation he previously passed across, pointing out the relevant information to the Judge who studies the papers, then:

(*Glowering at Toad*) Now listen to me: you are charged with stealing a valuable motor car. Driving to the public danger. Gross impertinence to the local constabulary. It's quite clear to me, Toad, that you are extremely guilty of all of these offences… (*To the Clerk*) What's the stiffest penalty that I can dole out to the unmitigated bounder?

Clerk He hasn't been tried yet, m'lud.

Judge I agree! I absolutely agree! He *should* be fried—and have his head boiled in oil too, I shouldn't wonder. Prisoner at the bar, you are aware, I take it, that you have the right to object to any member of the jury that doesn't meet with your approval?

Toad Yes, m'lud.

Judge And do you so wish to raise any objection?

Toad Yes, m'lud.

Again, the Wild-Wooders hiss and boo Toad

Judge (*banging his gavel*) Order! Order in court! Will the jury please rise.

The Wild-Wooders get to their feet

Now, prisoner, will you point out to the jury member to whose presence you object?

Toad I wish to object to all of them, m'lud.

Judge Eh? Eh? What's he say?

Clerk He wishes to object to all of them, m'lud.

Judge On what grounds?

Toad On the grounds that they're all objectionable!

The Wild-Wooders hiss and boo and, again, the Judge bangs his gavel. Badger is on his feet

Badger I believe, m'lud, that my client disapproves of the jury members because they are all Wild-Wooders.

Judge What's that? Do-gooders? What's wrong with do-gooders? Do you wish to call anyone to give evidence in the prisoner's defence?

Badger Yes, m'lud. I wish to summon the prisoner himself to take the stand.

Clerk Call Toad!

Constable Call Toad!

Clerk Take your place in the witness-box.

As the Constable escorts Toad to the witness-box, the Judge makes a great show of polishing his spectacles which he then replaces on his nose

Judge The prisoner may speak… (*He glances across at the dock and is horrified to discover that Toad is no longer there. He raps his gavel*) The prisoner's escaped! Lock all the doors! Search the entire building! The felon mustn't be allowed to get away! Summon the Constable!

The Clerk tugs at the Judge's sleeve and draws his attention to Toad who is standing in the witness-box—the Judge appears even more astounded

Merciful heaven! There's another of 'em! He's an uglier-looking blaggard than the last one!

Clerk He's there to give evidence on his own behalf, m'lud.

Judge Why? What's this one done? (*To Toad*) Speak up, fellow?

Song 11: Send Him Down

Toad (*singing*) I shouldn't be in this hole,
A Toad who has done no wrong,
A creature whose sheet is incredibly clean,
A person whose virtue is plain to be seen,
As straight as the day is long.

I shouldn't be in the dock,
I've tried to fight the good fight,
I've never transgressed and my conscience is clear
Will someone please tell me what I'm doing here?
I've always been whiter than white.

Badger He's right!

Judge Pooh, pooh! Same old story! I wish I'd a penny-piece for every time I've had to sit here and listen to that sort of rubbish!

Toad You mindless old magistrate! Call yourself a judge? You're not fit to judge a prize marrow in a village hall vegetable competition.

Judge You insolent creature! I'll see that you suffer for that remark!

The Wild-Wooders hiss and boo again and Toad shakes his fist at them

Toad As for you lot! You're none of you fit to be in a jury-box! I'd call this a kangaroo court—if it wasn't giving marsupials a bad name!

Badger Stop it, Toad! You're only making things worse for yourself.

Toad (*singing*) It couldn't get worse,

Badger He doesn't mean it, he's upset,

Toad Don't be so wet,
How could it get worse?
Things are as worse as worse can get...

Toad is overcome with a sudden wave of self-pity

Judge Return that snivelling creature to the dock!

The Constable escorts Toad back to the dock, as Badger continues

Badger M'lud, I'd like to call Water-Rat to the witness-box.

Clerk Call Water-Rat!

During the following, Rat moves to the witness-box

Judge What's that? Who's bought a hat? What's he bought a hat for?

Clerk Water-Rat, m'lud. To give a character reference on the accused' behalf...

Rat is now in the witness-box

Rat M'lud, may it please the court, I have known the accused for a number of years, and I don't think it's his fault—poor old Toady's never had a chance:

(*Singing*) He was pandered as a tadpole,
He was not taught wrong from right,
Toady isn't such a bad soul,
I beg mercy for his plight.
He had problems in his schooldays,
He was never good at logs,
He fell into stagnant pool ways,
With a crowd of yobbo frogs.

Clerk Frogs?

Rat Frogs.

(*Speaking*) ...In short, m'lud, I think it's all because of the way that he was brought up.

Judge Bought a cup? Who's bought a cup? There's one of 'em buying hats; another purchasing crockery—this is a court of law not a shopping mall! Stand down.

Wild-Wooders (*singing*) Send him down,
Send him down,
Send him down, down, down.
Make him pay,
All the way,
Send him down,
Make him squeal, make him croaky,
Put the rascal deep in chokey,
Let him drown,
Go to town,
Oh send him down!

Toad Who's in charge here? You or them? You silly old jumped-up judiciary!

Judge Be quiet, you aggravating amphibian, or I'll have you committed for contempt.

Badger Toad, behave yourself—or you really will be in trouble.

Toad I couldn't be any deeper in trouble than I am now.

He indicates the Wild-Wooders who are up on their feet and gesturing at him tauntingly

Look at them—they've got it in for me already. The jury's bent and, what's more...

(*Singing*) The Judge is barmy

Badger Pay no attention, it's distress——

Toad I'm not distressed,
You're being smarmy,

Badger He has suffered much duress.
M'lud, I'd like to call Mole to the witness-box.
Clerk Call Mole!

Mole goes to take Rat's place in the witness-box

Judge Who's this one?
Clerk Mole, m'lud. Another witness for the defence.
Mole Oh my, oh my!
Badger Take your time, Mole. Don't be afraid, old chum.
Mole M'lud, I'd just like to say... Oh my... I'd just like the court to know...
(*Singing*) There is not much I can add, sir,
To what Water-Rat has said,
Except that Toad's not bad, sir,
Just a trifle easily led.
I have only known him briefly,
But his ways I'm sure he'll mend,
I'd just say about him chiefly,
That I'm proud to call him friend.
Badger Well said, Mole.
Toad Thanks, Moley, old chap. I'll do the same for you some day.
Judge The prisoner will only speak when he's spoken to.
Wild-Wooders Give him time,
Give him time,
Give him time, time, time,
Let him dwell,
In his cell.
Give him time.
Send the villain off to prison,
He deserves to get what's his'n,
Give him time,
For his crime,
Oh give him time!

Still more exchanges between Toad and the Wild-Wooders

Judge Order in court! Order, order!
Badger Toad, for the last time—you're doing yourself irreparable harm!
Toad I couldn't care an owl's hoot, Badger. I don't stand a tadpole's chance in a jam-jar anyway.
(*Singing*) This court is rotten
Badger If my client's tones are fruity——
Toad They're not fruity
They're all spot on

Badger —it's because he feels his duty
Is to stand up straight, unflinching,
And to state it to the court
That he's sorry he went pinching,
Toad And I'm sorrier I got caught
Badger If you'll only treat him gently
Show some justice, just this time,
Toad won't touch another Bentley
He'll turn his back on future crime.

Clerk Crime?

Rat Crime.

Toad Justice, Badger? Mercy? Old misery-guts doesn't know the meaning of the word.

Judge One more word from you, you disgusting green creature, and you'll spend the rest of your days locked up!

Wild-Wooders Serve him right.
Serve him right.
Serve him right, right, right.
Say the word.
Give him bird,
Serve him right.
Make his stately home a hovel,
See him plead and watch him grovel,
Serve him right,
Well it might,
Oh serve him right!

Further gestures and insults between Toad and the Wild-Wooders

Judge Order! Order! This case has gone on longer than enough. Has the jury reached a verdict?

Wild-Wooders Yes, m'lud!

Judge And do you find the prisoner guilty or very guilty?

Wild-Wooders Very guilty!

Judge So do I. The prisoner will rise and face the court. On your feet, you snivelling wretch! It only remains for me to pass sentence——

Badger M'lud—if I may be allowed one last word?

Judge Oh, very well—if you must.

Badger We're all agreed, m'lud, that Toad committed all of these offences. He's admitted it himself. But as he's promised, faithfully, that he'll never again do anything of the kind—and taking into account the fact that he's never previously been up before the court—and considering that he's well-known all along the river bank for his kindness and good nature——

Judge Is that known to be a fact?
Clerk It is acknowledged to be so, m'lud.
Badger He wouldn't dream of walking by the river without a bag of breadcrumbs for the ducks, m'lud.
Company Awwww...!
Badger One winter, may it please the court, he took a fieldmouse with a broken paw into Toad Hall and kept it, safe and snug, until the spring.
Company Awwww...!
Badger On another occasion, m'lud, he cared for a baby hedgehog that had lost its mother and he nursed it, night and day, until it was fit to crawl along in the world.

By now the Judge, the Clerk-of-Court, the Constable, Mole and Rat are so moved by Badger's words that they are all weeping into their handkerchiefs

Don't you think, m'lud, that considering the circumstances, you might deal leniently with my client?
Judge Oh, very well. Now, pay attention, Toad—it had been my intention to come down on you extremely harshly, but as Badger has spoken so eloquently on your behalf, I'm going to let you off lightly.

Excitement in the court and consternation amongst the Wild-Wooders

Twenty-five years solitary confinement. Take him down, Constable.

Toad crumbles visibly. Rat, Mole and Badger engage in a concerned whispered conversation. The Wild-Wooders are jubilant. The Judge gathers his papers together, prior to leaving. Over all of which, there is a discordant chord from the orchestra, as the Lights fade

Scene 2

A Dungeon Cell

A gruesome skeleton is dressed in rags and chained to the wall

Toad, sobbing quietly to himself, is ushered into the cell by the Constable

Constable Now then, now then! Chin up, Toady. Things are never as bad as they seem, y'know.
Toad Aren't they?
Constable Not a bit of it. You'll like it here, once you've settled in. (*He*

gestures at the skeleton) Take your cell-mate there. Years and years he's been our guest and I can't remember when we last had a complaint from him. Don't cry, Toad—you'll wet your nice clean straw. Oh yes, it's all mod cons in here. Running water—all down the walls. Peace and quiet—except for the screams from the torture chamber. Hot meals every day—mustard sandwiches. Just my little joke, Toady. Your tea will be along now any minute. I'll get my niece to fetch it for you. I'll leave you to your thoughts.

The Constable exits

Toad sinks slowly to the floor

Toad Oh dear! It's the end of everything! It's certainly the end of me. The end of Toad. The popular and handsome Toad. The rich and hospitable Toad. Now I must languish in this deepest dungeon until all those that were proud to know me have forgotten my very name! Oh woe! Oh unfortunate amphibian! Oh woe... (*He dissolves into more tears, his head in his hands*)

Enid enters with a tray of food

Enid Why—what's all this? Tears at tea-time? This won't do! Sit up, dry your eyes and be a sensible creature.

Toad I can't! Oh, woe, woe, woe!

Enid Yes, you can—if you try! Come on, eat something. You'll feel better for it.

Toad Food, eh? I suppose I should try to keep my strength up.

Enid (*seeing his face for the first time*) Why—it's Mr Toad!

Toad Have we been properly introduced, young lady? Do I know you?

Enid I'm Enid. The housemaid...? At Toad Hall...?

Toad Do you know, I do believe I may have spotted you cleaning out the fire-grates and scrubbing floors. I say, is Hawkins hovering outside? You might ask him to bring me the *Financial Times*, a pot of tea and some toasted crumpets.

Enid Mr Hawkins isn't here, you funny creature. This is my day off. I popped over to see my uncle. He's the Constable. He asked me to bring you this. It's bubble-and-squeak. I made it myself.

Toad (*tasting the food*) Not bad—not quite the comforts of home though.

Enid You're in prison, Mr Toad. This *is* your home for now.

Toad Home? *Home*! My home is a highly desirable gentleman's residence, unique and dating in part from the fourteenth century. Five minutes from the church, the post-office and the——

Enid Bless you, Mr Toad, I know where Toad Hall is. I live there. It's my home too, remember.

Toad *Your* home? Your *home*! Toad Hall, Miss, is your place of employment—that hardly qualifies it as your home.

Enid The place that I call "home", is where I hang my best bonnet—which, at the time of asking, is on the hook behind the attic door on the top floor of Toad Hall. And that's the place I'm pleased to look upon as home—no matter what you might think. You don't have to own a place to turn it into home, Mr Toad

Toad You don't?

Enid Of course not! Home's where you find it. Home's ... well... Home's home...

Song 12: Home

(*Singing*)
Home is the place
You leave your heart in,
That certain space,
You made your start in.
A castle tall,
A cottage small,
Toad Perhaps a prison cell.
Enid The place you sleep,
A thought you keep,
That only you know well.

Home is not far,
The sky above you,
Seek out your star,
Someone to love you.
A place to stay,
A dream away.
It's there if you are strong.
Wherever's best,
Some special nest,
That's where you belong.

No matter where you wander,
Wherever you may roam,
You know that somewhere yonder,
There's a place you call home.

Home's where you stay,
It's what you make it,
Far, far away,
Never forsake it.

Home is for two,
For me and you,
Where we are, home is there,
Look to your heart,
Home's everywhere…

Toad (*visibly moved*) Are you going back to Toad Hall today?

Enid (*nodding*) Poor Mr Toad. I do feel sorry for you. Would you like to escape?

Toad Escape? Wouldn't I just! But I wouldn't stand a chance—this place is surrounded by guards. I counted them as I came in. Oh, woe, woe, woe!

Enid It might be possible. Listen to me, my aunt's a washerwoman.

Toad There, there—you mustn't blame yourself, Enid. I have several aunts who *ought* to be washerwomen.

Enid Do be quiet—and *listen*! She does all the washing for the prisoners, so she can come and go about these dungeons as she pleases. Supposing I borrowed some of her clothes?

Toad What's wrong with the ones you're wearing?

Enid Not for me. For you. You could put them on. You could escape in them.

Toad Me? Toad? Dress up as a washerwoman?

Enid Why not? You're very much like her in some ways.

Toad Don't be ridiculous.

Enid It's true—you *are*—particularly about the figure.

Toad I'll have you know, Miss, that I happen to have a very elegant figure—for what I am.

Enid So has my aunt—for what she is. But have it your own way. You horrid, proud, ungrateful creature. I was only trying to help you.

Toad I know, I know. You are a good, kind, clever girl—and I am a proud and vain and stupid Toad. But I am grateful for your help—and, yes, I'll do anything it takes to escape from here. Please—bring me the washerwoman's clothes.

Enid I'll be as quick as it takes.

Enid skips out

The Constable returns, on his rounds, and peeps in on Toad

Constable Cheer up, Prisoner Toad. The first twenty years are the worst. Ask your cell-mate. (*He gestures at the skeleton*) The days fly past so fast for him, he barely notices they've been and gone.

The Constable continues on his rounds

Toad considers the skeleton, and shivers. He is galvanised into action. He takes off his coat and waistcoat

Enid returns with a bundle of clothing

Enid Here! Quick! Put these on!

Toad and Enid ad-lib their dialogue as he struggles into: a corset, a pair of outsize bloomers, a cotton gown, an apron, a shawl and a black bonnet. During this, Enid fashions Toad's jacket and waistcoat into a washing bundle

Toad How do I look?
Enid (*giggling*) The spitting image of my aunt. No-one's going to recognize you. Go quickly—follow the path that you were brought in by. Look after yourself, Toad.
Toad (*pausing at the door to raise an exultant fist*) Ingenious Toad! Master of Disguise! You look after Toad Hall—perhaps I'll get back there—one day...

Enid watches Toad exit

Enid (*waving sadly*) Perhaps...

No matter where you wander,
Wherever you roam,
You know that somewhere yonder,
There's a place you call home.

Home is not far,
The sky above you,
Seek out your star,
Someone to love you.
Run hard, run fast,
And then at last,
You'll find your home is there,
Look to your heart,
Home's everywhere.

At the end of the number, the Lights fade as Enid exits and the stage clears

The Constable appears at one side of the darkened, empty stage, in a spotlight, blowing his whistle in short, sharp blasts: "Peep-peep! Peep-peep!" He is joined by a 2nd Constable, on the opposite side of the stage, also blowing a whistle in exactly the same manner. Two more Constables run on, shrugging on their uniform jackets

3rd Constable 'Ello, 'ello, 'ello? What's all this 'ere then?

1st Constable Toady's done a runner, lads.
4th Constable 'Ee's not broken out of that prison, 'as 'ee?
2nd Constable 'Ee 'as! Got clean away! After him, lads! We'll soon 'ave the blighter back where 'ee belongs!

As Toad takes flight into the auditorium, the four Constables, followed by a number of roving spotlights, pursue him this way and that, in a choreographed chase, blowing the "Peep-peeps!" on their whistles. Toad succeeds however in making good his escape

Scene 3

The Edge of the Wild Wood

Opening in darkness. A small circle of light appears—which brightens until we recognize it as the glow from a lantern. The light glows brighter and now, standing in its circle, we recognize Badger, Rat and Mole. Badger raises a paw to his mouth, in warning

Badger Ssshhh! We must be wary of the Wild-Wooders.
Mole (*glancing anxiously into the shadows*) But, Badger, how do you *know* that the Wild-Wooders are on the rampage?
Badger Because, Mole, as a respected senior animal around these parts, I'm expected to know. Believe you me, there's little that goes on in or around the Wild Wood that I don't know about. If a twig breaks. These sharp ears of mine hear it. If a tiny feather falls from a robin's nest, these keen eyes of mine observe it drifting to the ground. If the smallest of fieldmice should choose to tiptoe across the softest forest floor, this old nose of mine would have sniffed it out before it even stretched out a paw. That's how I know that the Wild-Wooders are on the rampage. My senses are attuned to pick up these things.
Mole (*impressed*) Oh my!
Rat (*not so impressed*) And his paws are attuned to pick up a newspaper, aren't they, Badger?
Badger (*stiffly*) I beg your pardon, Rat?

Rat takes a folded newspaper out of Badger's pocket

Rat (*unfolding the newspaper*) It's in *all* the newspapers. Right across the top of the front page in very big black letters: "Wild-Wooders On The Rampage!"
Badger (*even more stiffly*) I hadn't noticed it.

Rat (*to Mole*) They're rampaging around the entire countryside. It's high time somebody stood up to them.
Badger Perhaps somebody will. Perhaps, one of these fine days, somebody will give those Wild-Wooders the walloping they deserve.
Mole Hear hear, Badger! (*During the following, he peers at the bottom of the newspaper's back page which is level with his nose*)
Badger Quite. For the time being, however, we three must stick close together.
Rat (*glancing nervously into the shadows*) Badger's right. Particularly in dark and lonely places. It wouldn't do to be seen out singly.
Mole What's this bit down here about Toad?
Badger Toad? In the newspaper? Are you sure?

Rat turns the newspaper around and studies the relevant item

Rat Mole's right, Badger! There *is* a piece about Toad.
Badger Now that's something I hadn't read.
Rat (*reading*) "The irresponsible Mr Toad, who was recently sentenced to twenty-five years imprisonment, has perpetrated a cunning escape from his prison cell".
Badger Toad? Escaped? We must set out to find him.
Rat He's sure to need our help.
Badger Ratty, you set off in that direction: I'll go this way.
Mole What shall I do?
Badger You'd best keep guard here, Moley, old chap. Until we get back—either that or we'll all meet up again at Rat's place. Good hunting!
Rat We'll split up—good luck!

Rat and Badger go off in separate directions

Mole is left holding the lantern and the newspaper and full of trepidation

Mole (*calling off*) But Ratty—if we split up, can I come with you? Ratty? Badger? Why does it always have to be *me*…?

As Mole takes to his heels, the Lights fade to Black-out

Scene 4

The Canal Bank

In the cold grey light of dawn, we discover Toad curled up in the shelter of a tree, fast asleep and still wearing his washerwoman's clothing. All is still and silent. Toad shivers. Then, suddenly, the scene is flooded with sunlight. Toad sits up and rubs his eyes. A thrush sings out from a nearby hedge. Toad clambers to his feet, yawning

Toad Good morning, Mrs Thrush! Isn't it a glorious one too? Not only that, but I'm free! Free! Oh, inestimable morning! Inestimable Toad!

Song 13: Hello, World

(*Singing*) Hello world,
Good morning, morning,
A bright new day,
Has come my way,
Without a warning.
Hi there, sun,
How are you, blue skies,
This day and me,
We both agree,
You're a great sunrise.
Goodbye care,
So long to losing,
From here on in,
It's win, win, win.
I do the choosing,
Hello world,
Good morning, morning,
Just look at me,
I'm fancy free,
So hello world.

By the end of the first refrain, a number of animals, of all kinds, have appeared out of their hiding places: a couple of Rabbits, possibly the Fieldmice from ACT I, some Ducks, etc. All of them join in the next refrain:

Company On this morning,
This bright and carefree morning,
It's good to be,
Out here in the sunshine,
Every daybreak,
We're outside our front door.
Each day we make,
A country occasion,
Cause for celebration,

Summer's here,
Try it, taste it,
Appreciate don't waste it,
On this morning,
With all our flags unfurled,
Good-day new day,
Welcome to the world.

Which is followed by the two refrains sung in counter-point

At the end of the number, the stage clears except for Toad

The Pantomime Horse enters, pulling a barge on a tow-rope

Toad Hello, horse. (*He recognizes his old companion*) Black Beauty—it's you! How are you? Where have you been? (*He moves to pat the horse*)

Bargewoman, a formidable lady, enters, following the barge

Bargewoman Hey there! You, missis! Hands off! You leave my horse alone!

Toad *Your* horse? What cheek! This is *my* horse. I lost him. You stole him. You're mine, aren't you, boy?

The Pantomime Horse shakes its head

Thanks very much. He is mine. I'll prove it too—I'll tell you his name. Black Beauty.

Bargewoman Black Beauty? He's White Wonder. (*Aside*) Black Beauty indeed!

Toad (*aside*) White Wonder? The woman's colour blind.

Bargewoman *Your* horse. Why would a common person like yourself have need of a horse?

Toad Common person? *Me*? Are you aware, Bargewoman, of whom you are addressing?

Bargewoman I dunno *who* you are, ma'am—but I do know what you look as if you should be—a washerwoman.

Toad (*incensed*) A washer-wo—! (*He suddenly remembers that, at that moment, he is indeed adopting such a disguise and adopts a suitably servile attitude*) A washerwoman! Lawks a mercy, indeed I am, mum, I am indeed. And not only a common skivvy, mum, but one weighed down with more cares than a humble body cares to consider.

Bargewoman Why? Whatever's wrong?

During the following, the Bargewoman exits briefly and returns pushing a washtub on wheels and containing a washboard. The significance is lost on Toad

Toad Ah… If only I knew! That's it exactly—I'm on my way to find out. It's my married daughter. She sent for me to come to her at once. So off I comes, as any mother would, not knowing what may have happened, or be going to happen, but dreading the worst, as you will understand, mum, if you have children of your own—and bless you, mum, for your concern. And, as if that's not enough, I've lost all my money—to say nothing of losing my way, to boot.

Bargewoman Where might your married daughter be living, ma'am?

Toad Close by the river, mum—near to a fine house called Toad Hall. Perhaps you may have heard of it?

Bargewoman Toad Hall? Why, I'm headed that way myself—as soon as my chores are done. This canal joins the river a few miles on—and then it's an easy walk.

The Bargewoman goes off again and returns with a basket piled high with washing

I'll give you a lift if it will help?

Toad God shower you with blessings, mum, for your kindness to an old body.

Bargewoman A pleasure, I'm sure. So you're in the washing business? And a fine business you've got, I shouldn't wonder?

The Bargewoman again exits and this time returns with a large kettle which she sets by the tub

Toad (*his boastful self again*) Finest business you'll ever see—employed by all the gentry in the land.

The Pantomime Horse is shaking its head as a warning to Toad

Bargewoman Then let's see how much you know. How would you wash my smalls?

Toad Boil them first, until they were clean, then stretch them wide until they were big enough.

Bargewoman You're joking!

Toad Oh yes, yes, I am. As my late husband would have been pleased and proud to tell you, rest his soul: only let me get my head over a washboard, and my hands dipped deep in soapsuds—and I'm in my element.

He is aware, at last, of the Pantomime Horse's warning—but it is too late

Bargewoman A lucky chance my meeting you, then! Good fortune for the both of us.
Toad What do you mean?
Bargewoman Why, I'll take you down the river… (*She hands Toad the kettle*) If you can do my washing for me.
Toad Me? Can't you do the washing and let me steer the barge for you instead?
Bargewoman No.

The Bargewoman and the Pantomime Horse shake their heads in unison. Toad empties the kettle into the tub and clouds of steam rise up

Toad No?
Bargewoman No!

The Bargewoman gives Toad the washing and he dumps it in the tub. She hands him the washboard and he is plainly at a loss as to what to do with it

Toad Oh, no!
Bargewoman (*handing him a scrubbing-brush*) Oh, yes!

The Bargewoman hands Toad a bar of soap but it slips out of his hand, up into the air and then down into the canal—the orchestra pit. We hear the complaining "Quack-quack!" of a duck. The Bargewoman hands Toad a second bar of soap, with exactly the same result. A third bar of soap follows the route of the ones that have gone before—but this time it is thrown back at Toad. As he skips nimbly out of its path, he hoists his skirts, revealing his green legs

Ugh! What's them? Them's frog's legs! I've been watching you! I thought you was a humbug from the very start! You're not a washerwoman! You've never washed so much as a dish-cloth in your entire life! Clear off!

The Bargewoman wheels away the wash-tub, etc.

Toad (*calling after her*) Washerwoman indeed! I would have you know that I am Toad! *The* Toad! Master of Disguise! Escaper Extraordinaire! The Houdini of the Road Toad! The Inestimable Toad! A horse, a horse—my Toad-dom for a horse!

Toad clambers on to the back of the Pantomime Horse and rides off

The Bargewoman enters

Bargewoman Stop! Stop! Stop that Toad! (*She gives short, sharp tugs at the chain on the vessel's whistle which "Toot-toots" in a familiar manner*)

The four Constables rush onstage, blowing their whistles in a similar vein

Song 14: Peep-Peep

Constables Peep, peep,
Peep-peep,
Old Toad is out of gaol.
Peep, peep,
Peep-peep,
With all us coppers on his tail.
Peep, peep,
Peep-peep,
All together "there he goes!"
Secure that Toad,
Make sure that Toad,
Goes back to his dungeon deep.
And for his pains,
Is kept in chains,
So we can get some sleep,

Bargewoman He's clean away,
You'll never nab him,
He's far too clever by far to fall into your trap.

That so-and-so,
Just try and grab him,
He's free, you'll see,
The open road,
Belongs to Toad,
While you go,

Constables Peep, peep,
Peep-peep,
Old Toady's done a bunk.
He's burned his bridge, his boat is sunk.
Peep, peep,
Peep-peep,
All together find him now.
Search man-to-man,
Amphibian,

His goose we soon will cook.
Quick, catch that Toad,
Despatch that Toad,
And bring that Toad to book.

Quick, catch that Toad,
Despatch that Toad,
And bring that Toad to book.

Still blowing their whistles and colliding with each other in their excitement, the Constables exit in different directions, in search of Toad

Scene 5

Rat's House

It is neat and cosy and has a round earthen hole window through which can be seen the opposite river bank. There is a table which is laid out with a buffet meal

Rat is sitting on a keg sorting a pile of weaponry into three separate heaps

Rat Here's-a-sword-for-the-Mole, here's-a-sword-for-the-Badger, here's-a-sword-for-the-Rat! Here's-a-pistol-for-the-Mole, here's-a-pistol-for-the-Badger, here's-a-pistol-for-the-Rat! Here's-a-stick-for-the-Mole, here's-a-stick-for-the-Badger, here's-a-stick-for——

Toad's face appears at the hole in the wall. He is still dressed as a washerwoman and is soaking wet

—Toad! Toady, old chap—here, let me give you a hand. (*Grabbing Toad by the scruff of the neck, he drags him through the hole and into the living-room*) Where have you been? What have you been up to? And why on earth are you got up like that?

Toad Oh, Ratty! I've been through such times since I saw you last! Such trials, such sufferings, such escapes, such disguises, and all so nobly borne—and all so cleverly planned and carried out!

Rat And you're soaking wet—you're dripping all over my carpet.

Toad (*removing water-weed from his clothing*) That was all because of that stupid horse—it threw me in the river. Is that lunch? Good. I suppose I might just force down a mouthful—and then I'll stroll gently along to Toad Hall and collapse for a couple of weeks in my own comfortable bed.

Rat Stroll gently down to Toad Hall? Collapse into your comfortable bed? Do you mean to say that you haven't *heard*?

Toad Heard? Heard what, Ratty?

Rat Do you mean to stand there and tell me that you *don't know* about the Wild-Wooders?

Toad (*trembling*) What about the Wild-Wooders? What have they been doing?

Rat Why, they've taken over Toad Hall, of course! They're using it as their headquarters.

Toad Oh well, I'm done then. That's me finished. It's all over as far as I'm concerned.

Rat They moved in one dark night when it was raining cats and dogs. They crept quietly up the carriage-drive, armed to the teeth—you can't touch that boiled ham and beetroot salad—it's Badger's lunch. And the custard tart belongs to Mole.

Toad Oh! Oh, yes, of course! Moley and the Badger—what's become of those dear fellows?

Rat Well may you ask. While you've been gallivanting around the countryside, nobly bearing suffering and so forth, those two poor devoted animals have been camping in the open, in every sort of weather, watching over Toad Hall.

Toad What happened to my staff—aren't they responsible for the upkeep?

Rat Took to their heels, the lucky ones—or got booted out into the wind and rain when those wicked Wild-Wooders went in.

Toad (*half to himself*) Poor Enid…

Rat, puzzled, glances at Toad

(*Shrugging, by way of explanation*) …my housemaid—Toad Hall wasn't just her place of employment, Ratty, it was a roof over her head too…

Rat One thing's for certain—there's not a living soul left in there now, except for the Wild-Wooders—and Mole and Badger outside, hidden in the grounds, scheming and planning and contriving how to get your property back for you. (*He indicates the pile of weapons*) That's what this lot's all about.

Badger enters, beating his arms across his chest against the chill of the evening air

Badger (*gravely*) Welcome home, Toad. Alas, what am I saying? Home, indeed? This is a poor homecoming. Unhappy Toad. (*He crosses to the table where he sits, his back to the audience, eating his meal*)

Rat (*whispering*) Don't take any notice. He's always rather despondent when he's hungry.

Mole enters, also visibly feeling the cold, but he brightens on seeing Toad

Mole Hooray! Here's old Toad! Fancy having you back again, you clever, intelligent, ingenious Toad!

Toad (*boastfully*) Clever? Oh no, I'm not clever at all, according to some animals. (*A disparaging glance at Rat*) I've only broken out of the strongest prison in England, that's all. No, that's not all—I'll tell you some of my adventures, shall I——

Rat No, you shan't, Toad. And don't you egg him on, Mole—but please, tell us what the position is at Toad Hall?

Mole (*with a long sigh*) About as bad as it could be. They've got sentries posted everywhere. Guns poking out, stones throwed, windows barred, doors bolted...

During the following, they stop one by one as they realize that Badger has turned and is gazing at them severely

Rat We have to face facts—Toad Hall's impregnable. But I think I see now, in the depths of my mind, what Toad really ought to do. He needs to——

Mole No, he doesn't, Ratty! If you don't mind my saying so, what he ought to do is——

Toad Well, whatever it is, Moley, I shan't do it! So there! I'm not going to be ordered about by you fellows—it's Toad Hall we're talking about, and Toad Hall belongs to me, and——

Badger Be quiet—all of you! (*He rises slowly, and crosses to stand with his back to the fire, commanding attention*) Toad! You bad, troublesome little animal! Aren't you ashamed of yourself? *At all*? What do you think my old friend, your father, would have said had he been present tonight and knew of all your goings on?

Toad, seemingly full of contrition, bursts into tears

There, there. Stop crying. We're going to let bygones be bygones and try to turn over a new lily leaf, aren't we?

Toad But I haven't got a new lily leaf to turn over, Badger—or even an old lily leaf, come to that.

Badger Don't be so downhearted, Toad. What's needed now is courage. This is no time for tears—this is the time for action!

Song 15: Taken in Hand

(*Singing*) When a gang of wild Wild-Wooders start behaving out of hand,

When their code of conduct's frankly pretty poor,
Then it's up to upright animals to rise up across the land,
For we'll only take so much and then no more.

Mole
Rat } That's for sure!
Toad

Badger It's time someone cried "that's enough!"

Mole
Rat } Enough!
Toad

Badger High time some of us got in a huff,

Mole
Rat } Got tough.
Toad

Badger The need now's for action,
To get satisfaction,
We'll have to start playing it rough,

Mole
Rat } That's the stuff!
Toad

Toad (*crumpling immediately*) It's no good, Badger—what's the use of talk? There are only four of us against a whole army of them.

Rat Toad's right, for once, Badger. It'd be like trying to storm a fortress.

Badger There are more ways of capturing a castle, Ratty, than taking it by storm. I'm going to let you all in on a secret now. There—is—an—underground passage.

Toad Badger, I know every inch of Toad Hall. I was born there. I own it. Believe me, if there was any such thing as a secret passage, I'd be the first one to know about it.

Badger And you hear this, Toad—your father, who was a worthy creature, was a good friend of mine—and if he had wanted to keep anything a secret, you would have been the last one he'd have told. However, the time has come for you to know: there's an underground passage—it leads right up under the butler's pantry.

Toad The squeaky board in the butler's pantry—that would explain it!

Badger We shall creep up, without a sound, into the pantry——

Rat —with our pistols and swords and sticks——

Mole —and rush in on 'em——

Toad —and whack 'em and whack 'em and whack 'em——

All (*singing*) They've got to be walloped and whacked,
And whacked,
They need to be chastised and smacked,
We'll show them their station,

A good education,
Is something those rascals have lacked,
That's a fact!

The Lights fade

SCENE 6

The Secret Passage

Badger, Mole and Rat enter the dark confines of the passage, each of them holding a lantern aloft. Rat and Mole are armed to the teeth, with swords and pistols tucked into their belts, but Badger has need only for a stout stick

Badger Come on, then! We must be almost there. Follow me—Moley first.
Rat Why him?
Badger Because I'm very pleased with Mole. Ratty next, Toad last... Where *is* Toad?

Toad enters nervously and walking backwards

Toad I'm guarding the rear, Badger.
Badger Toad, if you can't keep up with the rest of us—you can jolly well go back now.
Toad Sorry, Badger.
Badger Come on! This way.
Rat Badger, you haven't brought the sword I chose for you—or the pistol.
Badger (*gripping his stick firmly*) I assure you, Ratty, we shall need nothing but these. Why, once we're inside that dining-hall, we'll wipe the floor with 'em in five seconds flat. I'd have managed the whole business myself, only I didn't wish to deprive you chaps of a little fun. Come on!

They set off again. Toad almost leaps out of his skin

Toad Yerks!
Badger Quiet!
Mole Quiet!
Rat Quiet!
Toad Quiet!
Badger Now what's all the fuss about?
Toad Sorry, Badger. But I saw a horrible long-legged spider.
Rat Really, Toad! Do pull yourself together! We're setting forth on a mission of great danger and derring-do. What chance do we stand of pulling off this

venture, if you're going to let a little incey-wincey spider scare you? Where was it anyway?

Toad Crawling up your collar.

Rat (*out-leaping Toad*) YERKS!

Badger Quiet!

Mole Quiet!

Rat Quiet!

Toad Quiet!

They set off again, Toad swinging his stick enthusiastically as he brings up the rear

I'll learn 'em to steal Toad Hall! I'll learn 'em, I'll learn 'em!

Badger Quiet!

Mole Quiet!

Rat Quiet!

Toad Quiet!

Rat In any case, Toad, you shouldn't say "learn 'em". It isn't good English.

Badger Will you shut up, Rat! And why are you continually nagging at Toad? What's wrong with his English? It's the same as what I use myself—and if it's good enough for me, it ought to be good enough for you.

Rat I'm very sorry, Badger. Only I think it ought to be "teach 'em", not "learn 'em".

Badger But we don't want to teach 'em, we want to learn 'em—*learn* 'em! Come on!

As they set off again, Rat, puzzled, murmurs to himself

Rat Learn 'em, teach 'em, teach 'em, learn 'em—?

Badger For the very last time, will you be quiet! I warn you, Rat, any more nonsense and you can go back too. Now hush, everybody. (*He puts his forefinger to his lips, giving them all a final warning*)

They set off again. It is Mole's turn to bring them to a quick halt

Mole Ssshhh!

Badger Not you too, Moley? Now what is it?

Mole Sorry, Badger—but I felt sure I heard something. It sounded like music.

Badger (*disbelievingly*) Music?

Mole Sorry, Badger—as if someone was having—well, having a party…

They all listen, hard, but to no avail. Badger shakes his head and frowns at Mole who hangs his head

…Sorry, Badger.

Badger No more talking. Anyone. We must be almost there now. Come on…

Rat
Mole (*together*) Toad!
Badger

Toad Oh yes—forward.

As they set off again, their lanterns disappearing into the darkness ahead, we realize that Mole was right, there is the sound of music which increases in volume

Scene 7

Toad Hall

The Wild-Wooders—the males in white tuxedos, the females in flapper costumes—are dancing a lively Charleston based on Talking To Toad *and which arrives at a hectic climax. As the Wild-Wooders regain their composure, the Chief Wild-Wooder, a "Godfather" figure, approaches a "stand" microphone, dabbing at his forehead with a snow-white handkerchief. He holds up his hands to stem their rapturous applause*

Chief (*taking a piece of paper from his pocket*) You're too kind. Gentlemen—ladies—I'm not gonna make a speech—I'm gonna read you a poem which I've composed in honour of our benefactor. (*He waves a hand to take in their opulent surroundings*) The guy who's given us all this. Mr Toad. (*He clears his throat, and reads, in Mafia-like tones*)

Toad took to the road in a limousine,
Gained a certain notoriety,
The Judge says "Hey!"
This guy's gotta pay
For his crimes against society,
The gang a.k.a. The Wild-Wooders,
They ain't lookin' for no excuse,
Fixed things easy-peasy,
Made Toad Hall a speak-easy,
With an offer Toad couldn't refuse!

The Chief Wild-Wooder's literary effort is greeted with even greater applause—upon which, the door bursts open and Badger, Mole, Rat and Toad enter, bearing sticks

Badger Attack 'em, lads! Up river-bankers and at 'em!
Rat Cometh the hour, cometh the Rat!
Mole A Mole! A Mole!
Toad Attack 'em and whack 'em!

And they fall upon their enemies. The fight with the Wild-Wooders is an orchestrated and choreographed battle. At the end of which the entire band of Wild-Wooders are routed and only Badger, Mole, Toad and Rat are left onstage

Badger There—I think, between us, we managed that quite nicely. It's given me rather an appetite. I want some grub, I do. Stir your stumps, Toad! We've got your place back for you, and you haven't offered us so much as a sandwich. Moley, there's a good chap, cut outside and see what's happened to their sentries…

Mole exits

Badger and Rat set about uprighting the furniture. Badger catches sight of Toad who, instead of doing as he has been told, is scribbling furiously in a notebook

Toad! Now what are you up to?
Toad Writing, Badger.
Badger I can see that! Writing what exactly?
Toad A guest list, for one thing.
Badger Guest list? What guest list?
Toad Of Very Important People. I thought, as we'd fought such a wonderful campaign, we ought to celebrate the victory in fine style. Instead of a sandwich, like you asked, I'm organising a banquet.

Badger and Rat exchange a frown

Mole enters

Mole It is all over. As soon as the ones outside heard the racket in here, they threw down their weapons and fled. I'm sure they'll behave themselves in future.
Badger I'm sure you're right. Well done, Moley. Toad—you said you were writing a guest list "for one thing". What's the other thing?
Toad (*with exaggerated innocence*) Nothing, Badger.

Rat snatches the notebook out of Toad's hand and is glancing at what is written there

Rat Well, I'm blowed!
Badger What is it?
Rat It's Toad's programme for the evening's entertainment. Listen to this: "Opening Address—to be delivered by Toad. Opening Speech—by Toad. There will be other speeches during the evening, also to be delivered by Toad and on a variety of subjects: Our Prison System, The Waterways of Old England, Horse-Riding for Fun and Profit, the Incredible Recapture of Toad Hall, by Toad and with some slight assistance from..."

Rat breaks off as he catches sight of Badger who is shaking his head, firmly, at Toad

Badger No, Toad.
Toad No speeches, Badger?
Badger No, Toad.
Rat Badger's right, Toad. You know very well that your speeches are all conceit and boasting and vanity and gross exaggeration and ... and...
Badger Hot air!
Mole It's for your own good, Toady.
Rat You've got to turn over that new leaf sooner or later—and now seems a splendid time to start.
Toad Not even a very short speech?
Badger No speeches at all. And no guest list.
Toad But if there aren't to be any speeches, and if there isn't to be a guest list—who's going to want to come to the banquet?
Badger There isn't going to be a banquet...

Toad's face falls

...Banquets are far too grand, Toad. What's wrong with a simple honest-to-goodness, no-nonsense, take-us-as-you-find-us party?
Mole Oh yes! Oh my! And instead of Very Important People, Toady, you can invite all your friends.
Toad I haven't got any friends—apart from you chaps, of course.
Badger Absolute rot, Toad! And if you'd only see sense and stop trying to behave in the grand manner, you might just discover that you've got more friends than you ever dreamed possible.
Mole It's true, Toady. Perhaps if you showed a little kindness and friendship towards them, even the Wild-Wooders might turn into decent animal beings.
Rat You might begin, Toad, by not thinking of this place as Toad Hall—but just by calling it home.
Mole Toad's home.

Toad Toad's ... home?

Badger That's what the party's going to be about—Toad's homecoming.

Toad (*warming to the thought*) Toad's home. I've got a home. Would you like to see my home? Come in and put your feet under the table—warm your toes in front of the fire. Welcome to my home...

During the following, Enid enters, wearing a bonnet and an outdoor coat and carrying her possessions in a carpet bag

Song 16: Home (Reprise)

All Wherever you may wander,
Wherever you roam,
You know that somewhere yonder,
There's a place you call home——

During the following, the entire Company enters, bringing either presents for Toad or platters containing food for the party

Enid Home's where you stay,
It's what you make it,
Just for today,
Reach out and take it.

As Enid sings the next lines, the Company hum along with her

Enid Run hard, run fast,
And then at last,
You'll find your home is there,
Company Look to your heart,
Home's everywhere...

From which we segue into a rumbustious closing chorus

Song 17: Hello World (Reprise)

Hello world,
Good-morning, morning,
A bright new day,
Has come my way,
Without a warning.
Hi there, sun,
How are you, blue skies,

This day and me,
We both agree,
You're a great sunrise.
Goodbye care,
So long to losing,
From here on in,
It's win, win, win,
I do the choosing,
Hello world,
Good morning, morning,
Just look at me,
I'm fancy free,
So hello world.

Just look at me,
I'm fancy free,
So hello world!

Repeat with counterpoint

CURTAIN

FURNITURE AND PROPERTY LIST

Further dressing may be added at the director's discretion

ACT I

Scene 1

On stage: The River Bank

Off stage: Rowing-boat with oars, picnic hamper (**Water-Rat**)
White apron, whitewash brush (**Mole**)

Scene 2

On stage: Toad's Estate
3 garden chairs
Garden table
Gypsy caravan with shafts and straps
Jug of lemonade
Glass

Off stage: Picnic hamper (**Water-Rat, Mole**)
Glowing campfire (**SM**)

Personal: **Pantomime Horse:** bridle

Scene 3

On stage: The Open Road

Personal: **Toad:** overcoat, cap, goggles, scarf

Scene 4

On stage: The Wild Wood
Trees
Snow

Buried under snow: door-scraper, doormat, door with brass plate and bell-pull, light above door

Off stage: Brace of pistols, cudgel (**Rat**)

Personal: **Rat:** handkerchief

SCENE 5

On stage: OUTSIDE TOAD HALL
Ornate front door with brass knocker
Lighted lantern

Off stage: Duster (**Hawkins**)
2 empty milk bottles (**Hawkins**)
Stick (**Badger**)

Personal: **Toad:** motoring gear, cigar

SCENE 6

On stage: TOAD'S BEDROOM
Four-poster bed with bedding
Chairs
Fireplace

Personal: **Rat:** pocket-watch

SCENE 7

On stage: TOAD'S BEDROOM
As Scene 6, plus:
Toad's goggles and motoring cap under pillow, knotted sheets under eiderdown
Key in door

Off stage: Towels (**Badger**, **Rat**)

SCENE 8

On stage: THE VILLAGE

Off stage: Notebook, pencil (**Constable**)
Car (**Toad**)
Car wheel (**SM**)

ACT II

Scene 1

On stage: The Courtroom
Dock. *In it*: stool
Jury-box
High table and chair. *On table*: gavel
Desk and chair. *On desk*: quill pen, parchment document

Personal: **Judge:** spectacles, handkerchief
Badger: wig, gown
Clerk-of-Court, **Constable**, **Mole**, **Rat:** handkerchiefs

Scene 2

On stage: A Dungeon Cell
Skeleton in rags, chained to wall
Straw on floor

Off stage: Tray of food (**Enid**)
Bundle of clothing: corset, bloomers, gown, apron, shawl, bonnet (**Enid**)
Uniform jackets (**3rd** and **4th Constables**)

Personal: **Constables:** whistles

Scene 3

On stage: The Edge of the Wild Wood

Off stage: Lighted lantern (**Mole**)

Personal: **Badger:** folded newspaper

Scene 4

On stage: The Canal Bank
Tree

Off stage: Barge on tow-rope (**Pantomime Horse**)
Washtub on wheels, washboard (**Bargewoman**)
Basket with washing, 3 bars soap (**Bargewoman**)
Large kettle (**Bargewoman**)
Bar of soap thrown at **Toad** from orchestra pit (**SM**)

Personal: **Pantomime Horse:** bridle
Constables: whistles

SCENE 5

On stage: RAT'S HOUSE
Chairs
Table laid with food
Keg
Pile of weapons
Carpet
Fireplace

Personal: **Toad:** water-weed

SCENE 6

On stage: THE SECRET PASSAGE

Off stage: Lighted lanterns (**Badger**, **Mole**, **Rat**)
Swords, pistols, sticks (**Rat**, **Mole**, **Toad**)
Stick (**Badger**)

SCENE 7

On stage: TOAD HALL
Banqueting table. *On it*: remnants of feast, glasses
Chairs
Microphone

Off stage: Weapons (**Badger**, **Mole**, **Rat**, **Toad**)
Carpet bag (**Enid**)
Presents, platters of food (**Company**)

Personal: **Chief Wild-Wooder:** handkerchief, piece of paper
Toad: notebook, pencil

LIGHTING PLOT

Property fittings required: glowing campfire (I, 2), lamp above **Badger**'s door (I, 4), lanterns (I, 5 and II, 3 and 6)
Various simple interior and exterior settings

ACT I, Scene 1

To open: Moonlight, starry-sky effect

Cue 1 **Rat** enters in a rowing-boat (Page 1)
Bring up lighting on **Rat**

Cue 2 **Enid** exits (Page 2)
Bring up sunshine

Cue 3 **Mole**: "Who should interfere with him?" (Page 3)
Decrease sunny lighting as cloud passes over sun, return to previous lighting after whispered chorus

Cue 4 At and of Song 2, boat moves down river (Page 5)
Fade to black-out

ACT I, Scene 2

To open: Sunshine

Cue 5 **Toad**, **Rat** and **Mole** move off with caravan (Page 12)
Dim lights as night falls, bring up starry-sky effect and glowing campfire

Cue 6 **Rat** and **Mole** join **Toad** in slumber (Page 13)
Fade to black-out

ACT I, SCENE 3

To open: Early morning light

Cue 7 **Toad**'s "Poop-poops" fade into distance (Page 17)
Fade to black-out

ACT I, SCENE 4

To open: Wintry dusk lighting

Cue 8 **Rat**: "…and my friend Mole." (Page 22)
Snap on light above **Badger***'s door*

Cue 9 **All**: "For we're top grade." (Page 24)
Fade to black-out

ACT I, SCENE 5

To open: Moonlight, orange glow from lantern

Cue 10 **Enid** exits (Page 27)
Fade to black-out, then up to morning lighting

Cue 11 **Badger** & **Rat** & **Mole**: "So we should!" (Page 29)
Fade to black-out

ACT I, SCENE 6

To open: General interior lighting

Cue 12 **Toad** punches the air (Page 32)
Fade to black-out

ACT I, SCENE 7

To open: General interior lighting

Cue 13 **Toad** escapes through window (Page 36)
Fade to black-out

ACT I, SCENE 8

To open: General exterior lighting

No cues

ACT II, SCENE 1

To open: General interior lighting

Cue 14 **Judge** gathers his papers prior to leaving (Page 47)
Fade to black-out

ACT II, SCENE 2

To open: Dim interior lighting

Cue 15 **Enid**: "Home's everywhere." (Page 51)
Fade to black-out

Cue 16 When ready (Page 51)
Snap up follow spots on **1st Constable**, *then on* **2nd, 3rd** *and* **4th Constables**

Cue 17 **Toad** pursued by **Constables** in auditorium (Page 52)
Follow with roving spotlights, then snap off spots to black-out

ACT II, SCENE 3

To open: Black-out

Cue 18 When ready (Page 52)
Bring up **Mole**'*s lantern, slowly increase to circle of light on* **Badger**, **Rat** *and* **Mole**

Cue 19 **Mole** takes to his heels (Page 53)
Fade to black-out

ACT II, Scene 4

To open: Cold grey dawn lighting

Cue 20 When ready (Page 54)
Bring up sunlight

Cue 21 **Constables** exit (Page 59)
Fade to black-out

ACT II, Scene 5

To open: Warm, cosy interior lighting

Cue 22 **All**: "That's a fact!" (Page 63)
Fade to black-out

ACT II, Scene 6

To open: Black-out

Cue 23 **Badger**, **Mole** and **Rat** enter with lighted lanterns (Page 63)
Bring up dim interior lighting

Cue 24 **Badger**, **Mole**, **Rat** and **Toad** set off again (Page 65)
Fade to black-out

ACT II, Scene 7

To open: Bright interior lighting

No cues

EFFECTS PLOT

ACT I

Cue 1 To open Scene 1 (Page 1)
Mist effect, owl hoots nearby

Cue 2 To open Scene 3 (Page 13)
Birdsong

Cue 3 **Rat**: "Wait a minute, Toady!" (Page 13)
Engine-roar of fast-approaching car, accompanied by "poop-pooping" of horn, crash, then car roaring quickly into distance

Cue 4 **Rat** pulls bell-pull (Page 22)
Jangling a long way off

Cue 5 **Toad** drives on and off in his car (Page 39)
Roar of car, followed by horrendous crash

ACT II

Cue 6 **Toad** sits up and rubs his eyes (Page 54)
Thrush sings

Cue 7 **Toad** empties kettle into tub (Page 57)
Clouds of steam rise up from tub

Cue 8 **Toad** drops soap into canal (orchestra pit) (Page 57)
Complaining "Quack-quack!" of duck

Cue 9 **Toad** drops 2nd bar of soap (Page 57)
Repeat Cue 8

Cue 10 **Bargewoman** tugs at the chain of whistle (Page 58)
Toot toots in succession

MADE AND PRINTED IN GREAT BRITAIN BY
LATIMER TREND & COMPANY LTD PLYMOUTH
MADE IN ENGLAND